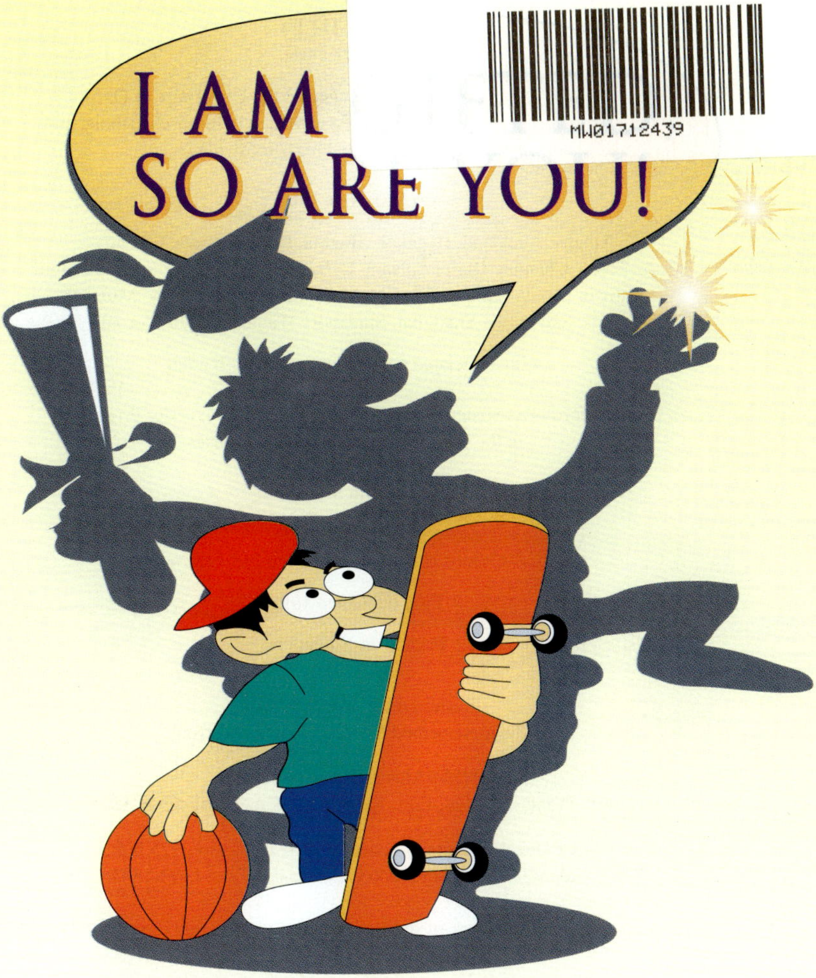

ADAM KHOO

WITH FOREWORDS BY
TONY BUZAN & ERNEST WONG

SINGAPORE
OXFORD UNIVERSITY PRESS

OXFORD
UNIVERSITY PRESS

Oxford University Press is a department of the University of Oxford.
It furthers the University's objective of excellence in research, scholarship,
and education by publishing worldwide in

Oxford New York

Athens Auckland Bangkok Bogotá Buenos Aires Calcutta
Cape Town Chennai Dar es Salaam Delhi Florence Hong Kong Istanbul
Karachi Kuala Lumpur Madrid Melbourne Mexico City Mumbai
Nairobi Paris São Paulo Shanghai Singapore Taipei Tokyo Toronto Warsaw

with associated companies in Berlin Ibadan

Published in Singapore
by Oxford University Press Pte Ltd

First published 1998

Printed in Singapore

Illustrated by Kenneth Wong
and supplemented by images obtained from:

IMSI's Masterclips Collection,
1895 Francisco Blvd. East, San Rafael, CA 94901-5506, USA

Nova Development Corporation's Art Explosion 125,000,
23801 Calabasa Road, Suite 2005. Calabasas, CA 91302-1547 USA

ISBN 0 19 588425 6

7 9 10 8 6

DEDICATION

Dedicated to the genius within you

Most of all, from me to my parents Vince, Betty and Joanne, my grandparents, my sister Vanessa, my family and Sally.

ACKNOWLEDGEMENTS

No worthwhile project can ever come into being without the combined effort of a team of talented individuals. Therefore, I need to thank many wonderful people for their invaluable contributions and for making this book a reality:

My parents for their support and comments on the manuscript; Kenneth Wong for his beautiful illustrations.

Heartfelt thanks also go out to Tony Buzan, Dilip Mukerjea and Vanda North, for their faith and support.

This book is also, in no small part, due to some very inspiring educators whose personalities, talents and friendship have influenced me profoundly on my journey. Thanks to Ernest Wong for being the first to tell me that I am gifted; Dr. Tad James and all the good people at Advanced Neuro Dynamics who introduced me to the world of NLP; then to Jerry Low, Stuart Tan and Joel Lee who taught me how to master NLP; finally to four giants of personal development, Dr. Richard Bandler (co-developer of NLP™ and developer of DHE™), Robert Dilts, Anthony Robbins and Eric Jensen.

I also thank all the academics who have helped shape my beliefs and attitudes; Prof. Wee Chow Hou and Dr. Kulwant Singh for their support and interest in my work; also all the other dynamic lecturers at NUS.

Going back further, I must thank the dedicated teachers and Principals of Ping Yi Secondary School (1987–90) who did not give up on me: Mrs. Ng Gek Tiang, Mrs.

Pearl Goh, Mr. Heng, Miss Grace Lee and Mdm. Markati Yusoff. Other people I must thank are Mrs. Lee Phui Mun (Principal), Ms Phua Puay Shan and teachers at Victoria Junior College (1991–92).

My gratitude also goes out to my friends and Super-Teen® Resource colleagues for powerful and memorable times at our camps; in particular, thanks go to Ms.Theresa Wong, Mr. and Mrs. Lee Say Keng, Jo Pang, Gary Tan, Tan Minyi, Zachary Low, Kenneth Wong, Audrey Ng, Audrey Tan, Eunice Lee and Mark Tan .

A special thank you to Patrick Cheo, Eric Ng, Benny Lee and Koh See Kwang for their dedication in helping me build up Creatsoul Entertainment and with whom I have had a lot of fun working. Also, thanks go out to Jack Tan and the staff of Razes Entertainment for supporting us all the way!

More special thankyous, this round to Dr. Tony Tan and Mrs. Mary Tan, who introduced my father to the Super-Teen® Programme and to Mr. Andrew Tan for his great faith in me. Others who believed in me and whom I must thank are Jeffery Chin and the ninth and tenth Management Committee (Faculty of Business Administration, NUS) for giving me the opportunity to conduct my courses there.

This book is also dedicated to my good friends Zeng Guangwei, Freddy Gomez, Tan Teck Wah, Steve Ang, Victor Ho, Ng Soo Ann, Ng Soo Gin, Ng Soo Ming, Low Zhi Peng, Eugene Tan, Kimmie Leong, Andrew and Evonne Wee, Catherine Ho, Shirley Chew, Dennis Yap, Tan Lye Poh, Kom Mun Sun and Melvyn Lu.

Finally, I must thank my army buddies for some unforgettable experiences, in particular, Maj Peter Wee (CO), Lta Jonathan Neo, Lta Koh Boon Tih, Lta(NS) Kenneth Tay, Lta(NS) Dhar Roopesh Coomer, Lta(NS) Sathia Moorthy, Lta Willy Lee, Lta Chris Ong, Cpt Lim Kok Siong, Cpt Ragunathan, Lta(NS) Benson Soh, Cpt Pang Choon Meng, Lta Ernest Ng, Cpt Joab Ang, Lta Lim Chen Jye, Cpt S. Amudhan, SSG Dilwant Singh and the men of Alpha Coy (1994–95), 165 SADA.

ABOUT TONY BUZAN

Tony Buzan, holder of the world's highest 'Creativity IQ', is the originator of Mind Mapping®, Founder of The Brain Trust, Chairman of the Brain Foundation and developer of the concept of Mental Literacy™.

He is one of the world's most consistent best selling authors, having written and published, more than twenty books on the brain, creativity, and learning, and one volume on poetry. To date, Mr. Buzan's books have been translated into over twenty languages and published in over fifty countries. His classic bestseller, *Use Your Head*, has sold over one million copies worldwide.

Tony Buzan is also a much sought-after speaker, having been rated by Forbes (USA) as one of the top lecturers in the world, along with such personalities as Margaret Thatcher and Henry Kissinger.

He is also a Fellow of the Institute of Training and Development and an elected member of the International Council of Psychologists. In addition, he is an advisor to international Olympic coaches and athletes and to the British Olympic Chess Squad.

Most recently, Tony Buzan, along with Raymond Keene, organized the first-ever Mind Sports Olympiad at the Royal Festival Hall, London (August 1997). Such activities are all part of Tony Buzan's dedication to helping people unleash more of their brain power. He has unquestionably influenced millions of people all over the world in the way they approach thinking and intelligence.

ABOUT ERNEST WONG

Ernest Wong became the first Malaysian and among the top one hundred people in the world to become a Certified Trainer in Accelerated Learning at Turning Point in the University Of California (USA). He is also a Licenced Practitioner of Neuro-Linguistic Programming™ certified by the Society of NLP™ (USA) at the University of British Columbia, Canada.

Mr. Wong is the Founder, Principal Counsultant and Master Teacher of Ernesco, the largest chain of motivational language learning centres, based in Kuala Lumpur, Malaysia. He has used his skills to successfully train more than twenty thousand students to speak languages over an accelerated period.

In 1985, he founded the Super-Teen® Programme, an accelerated learning and personal development course that utilises the most relevant techniques in Neuro-Linguistic Programming, Whole-Brain Learning, Suggestopedia, Edu-Kinesiology and Multiple Intelligence theory to teach students. The programme was the first of its kind in Asia and has transformed more than ten thousand ordinary students in Singapore, Malaysia, Hong Kong, China and Indonesia into peak performers.

In 1988, Mr. Wong became the first Asian to receive the Golden Apple Award for his contributions towards excellence in education. The award was given by the Foundation of Self Esteem in California (USA).

ABOUT THE AUTHOR

Adam Khoo is a final-year honours undergraduate in the Faculty of Business Administration at the National University of Singapore (NUS) (1997/1998). He is a Licenced Master-Practitioner and Trainer of Neuro-Linguistic Programming™, certified by the Society Of NLP™ (USA); and a Practitioner of Time Line Therapy™ certified by the Time Line Therapy Association (USA).

He ranks among the most outstanding students in NUS (1997/1998). He is in the prestigious Talent Development Programme (TDP), representing the top one percent of academic achievers, and has been placed on the Dean's Honour List every year for outstanding academic achievements.

Adam Khoo is also a trainer in the Super-Teen® Programme of Ernesco Genius Research Center Sdn Bhd, and Ernesco Pte Ltd. He has, together with Ernest Wong, successfully trained over four thousand students using the combined techniques of Neuro-Linguistic Programming, Accelerated Learning and Whole-Brain Learning.

Adam Khoo conducts training in Singapore and the ASEAN region. He has trained people from all walks of life at the National University Of Singapore, the St. Peter and Paul Church (Singapore), the Association Of Muslim Professionals (Singapore), University Harapan (Jakarta), the Chinese High School (Singapore), the Chinese Development Assistance Council (Singapore), Nanyang Girls High School (Singapore) and many other institutions and organizations.

He has written a series of motivational columns for *Teenage* magazine (Singapore). He is also the founding partner of Creatsoul Entertainment, an event management company. In addition, he serves as an honorary advisor to the Genius Students Circle (Singapore).

FOREWORD *BY TONY BUZAN*

It is a particular pleasure for me to write the foreword to Adam Khoo's *I Am Gifted, So Are You.*

His title is correct. He is gifted! This does not need to be proven in any other way for you than by reading the book which you now hold in your hands. Every page glistens with intelligence, humour, wit and creativity. What is particularly interesting about Adam's personal case is that for many years of his life, 'gifted' was not a term that was regularly applied to him, thus my even greater pleasure in recommending this book to you. On my lecture tours around the world, focusing on the development of human intelligence and the creation of thinking and learning organizations, one of the first things I talk about are the stories of those who were 'delinquent' or 'poor students', 'slow', 'backward', 'naughty', 'wicked', 'bad', 'educationally subnormal', 'disruptive', 'suffering from Attention Deficit Disability Syndrome', 'not destined for university', 'failures', 'dunces' etc.

My case has always been that the inherent intellectual capacity and basic creative brilliance of all human beings is far greater than we have ever thought and have regularly been told about.

It is wonderful therefore when an individual who is deeply ensconced in the 'non gifted' camp for some extraordinary reason, finds his or her way to the 'gifted' camp.

The way in which this gigantic and apparently impossible leap is made is virtually always through self-realization. Self-realization is also always nearly based on learning how the brain and the body work individually and in concert. This includes, almost obviously, learning about the fundamental nature of memory, thinking, creative thinking, reading and learning, while finding out about the fundamental, physiological and biological operations of the brain and the body.

Enter Adam!

From being a twelve-year-old 'non gifted', Adam, by learning about himself and especially learning how to learn, within a very short period of time, as you will find out when you read his personal story in Chapter One, graduated from being near the bottom of a class of students who were at the bottom of all the other classses, to being in the top ten percent, then in the top five percent, next in the top one percent. He did this not only on a short-term basis, but year after year after year.

FOREWORD *BY ERNEST WONG*

It is with great pride and excitement that I write this introduction to Adam Khoo's book. I was first introduced to this young man in 1987. Back then, he was an under-achieving thirteen-year-old who had been most unfortunately labelled a 'hopeless learner' by many people around him. Adam's parents had enrolled him in my programme, hoping that I could somehow make a better student out of him. They didn't have high expectations. Certainly they did not expect that within one short year Adam would become an outstanding student. When he did, I was thanked for having achieved nothing short of a miracle.

Well, I did not 'transform' Adam at all. In fact, I never have and never will be able to 'transform' anyone. What I simply and sincerely did was to offer Adam, as I offer all my students, greater choices in the way he could live his life. He could live it as a failure or as a success. My job was merely to teach him the skills and strategies he needed to create his own 'transformation'. The choice was entirely his.

Adam, like many other students who have gone through the Super-Teen® programme, chose the path to success. He used the strategies I had taught him but not only did he apply them with enthusiasm, but took them ten steps further. He underwent additional training and did his own research into the realms of Whole-Brain Learning, Accelerated Learning and Neuro-Linguistic Programming. He then used his expanded knowledge to test the strategies and put them to use in various areas of his life. The results Adam produced and continues to produce are nothing short of spectacular.

I am most gratified that the once 'under-achieving' teen is now an outstanding undergraduate and has, all these years, found the time to come back and join me in training new students in the Super-Teen® programme. Adam has served on the council of the Genius Student Circle, first as Vice-President for special projects, then as Deputy President, then as President and finally, as Honorary Advisor.

This book, is the product of his eleven years of applied knowledge, challenging experiences and exciting experimentation. He embodies what I would call 'true genius' of the Super-Teen® training programme. What is so unique about Adam's work is that it is written not only from the perspective of a remarkable trainer but also from that of a true practitioner of the work.

I believe that regardless of whether you are a student, a teacher or a parent and wherever you may be, here in Singapore, in Malaysia or even in the UK, this book could be worth a million 'A's to you.

CONTENTS

CHAPTER 1

'A' STUDENTS, A DIFFERENT BREED?

JUST ANOTHER UNDERACHIEVER

In every class, in every school, there is almost always a handful of very bright students, the 'A' scorers, a breed apart from the rest. During all of my primary school years, I was one of the 'rest', for whom the grades of the top students seemed quite unattainable.

That was the way my parents and my teachers saw me, and it was also the way I saw myself. In short, I was a 'below average student', who might have been able to do a bit better if only I 'weren't so lazy, so indifferent and such a TV addict.'

Certainly, no one ever imagined that I would amount to anything. Sounds familiar? Sounds like you? Well, I surprised everyone, even myself, so do read on and you could even surprise yourself!

But back then in 1987, no one was surprised when the Primary School Leaving Examination (PSLE) results were announced and I didn't even do well enough to make it to the secondary schools my parents listed as their preferred choices. I was despatched to Ping Yi Secondary school, a relatively new school no one we knew had heard of.

While I was not expected to suddenly shine at this new school, no one expected that I would backslide so far that my exasperated Secondary One Mathematics teacher would call my mother to ask why I could not even remember what I had been taught in Primary Four! At that time, I was ranked among the last ten students in my entire cohort of over one hundred and sixty students.

My parents responded like typical concerned parents and engaged yet another private tutor! It did not help one bit. I responded with lacklustre grades in all my subjects.

THE SUPER-TEEN® TURNING POINT

It was at the lowest ebb of my school career that my father learned of a special five-day residential programme for teenagers designed to teach them how to study and take charge of their lives. Deciding that they had nothing to lose, except their money, my parents enrolled me for the Super-Teen® Camp.

So, on a Sunday morning in March 1987, I was dropped off at the Ladyhill Hotel and put under the charge of Master Trainer Ernest Wong. I was a mere thirteen-year-old among forty other students aged between twelve and twenty.

On that day, I was far from thrilled about going to the camp but at the end of the five days, I was a completely changed teenager. The camp transformed my whole attitude and outlook, and I have never looked back since.

What brought about this complete transformation in personality was what Ernest Wong shared with us. Using American-developed learning technologies such as Accelerated Learning, Neuro-Linguistic Programming™ (NLP) and Whole-Brain Learning and adapting them for students, Ernest completely transformed our beliefs about what was possible. He showed us that everyone, even the most mediocre students among us, had the potential to be geniuses and leaders. The only things holding us back were our negative mental states and disempowering beliefs.

Intrigued and challenged, I left the camp with newly acquired Super Learning Tools, ready to claim my birthright. For the first time in my life, I set my sights on getting straight 'A's.

ACTION....WITH 'A' GOALS AHEAD

Back home and in school, I swung into action. Up went the self-drawn motivational posters on my walls. Within three months, I had pulled my grades up from an average of fifty-two percent to seventy percent. This enabled me to rise from one hundred and fifty-eighth position to being among the top eighteen, all in one memorable year, 1987.

From there I went on to top my school in the GCE 'O' Level Examinations with six distinctions and was admitted to the junior college of *my* choice, Victoria Junior College. In the 'A' Level Examinations, I scored three 'A's and after National Service, I entered the National University of Singapore to study for a Bachelor of Business Administration degree (BBA).

Starting from the first year of university, my grades earned me a place on the Dean's list (honor roll) and also a place in the NUS Talent Development Programme (TDP). The latter is a programme offered to the the top one percent of students at the University.

I achieved all this not as a 'mugger' but as a student who still found time to run a profitable event-management business (Creatsoul Entertainment, which was featured in the *Teenage Magazine* of June 1997) with several fellow undergraduates. In addition, I spent much of my after-school time as Executive Trainer in the Super-Teen® Programme, helping thousands of students to unleash their true genius.

IF I CAN...SO CAN YOU!

Yes, you can do it too, not necessarily by taking the same path, for you have your special talents just waiting to be tapped. It's true. No matter how badly you are doing now, no matter how many times you have failed, your potential for improvement is phenomenal.

I strongly believe that if a person like me, once labelled a 'bum' by some of my teachers, can turn around to achieve consistently good results, then you can too. Remember, I have been down there, at the bottom, so I understand your feelings and your needs. I want to share all I have learned because the journey of self-discovery is the most exciting one anyone can embark on.

SUPERSTARS AND 'SLOW' STUDENTS: SAME BRAIN, DIFFERENT STRATEGIES

Firstly, understand that it is not our inherent abilities and limitations that set us apart from the 'superstar' students; rather, it is the study techniques used by these students that gets them excellent results.

You and almost every student on the planet basically have the same type of brain and nervous system. Why then can some students read a page of chemistry once and apply the facts learnt to the examination questions while you struggle to recall even a vague description of what you have read? The reason is that they have learnt to use their brains in certain ways that allow them to access a greater portion of its learning power.

In short, they have learned *how* to learn whereas you have not.

If it's possible for others, it's possible for me.
It's only a matter of acquiring the right skills and strategies.

LEARN HOW TO LEARN

Are you baffled by this concept of 'learning how to learn'? Well, consider this. Aren't we all in the habit of taking lessons on swimming, golf, tennis, sailing or wind surfing before being allowed to 'play'? 'Yes', you say. Then how is it that all of us are sent school to do well in learning and tested through examinations when we have never been taught how to study?

We have never been taught memory skills or how to take notes intelligently and we were certainly not taught examination strategies, yet we were all expected to perform well in school.

Isn't it all very unfair? How can we be expected to learn if we were never taught *how* to learn?

In this book, you will learn how to learn.

THE GAME OF EXAMINATIONS

ARE YOU GAME?

One student fully understands the concepts of a subject passionately and even knows how to apply that knowledge yet he is rewarded with a 'C' average. Another has a more shallow understanding of that same subject, yet scores an 'A'. Why? The answer is that the second student knows the rules of the game of examinations whereas the first does not.

This knowledge of the rules of examinations will enable you to score the highest marks in a paper that is between two and three hours. It is simply knowing how to give the marker what he or she wants to see in a very short time so that the marker is totally convinced that you are competent in that subject. If you do not know the rules of the examination game, you will not come out on top.

The first step in learning the rules of the game is to understand how to learn.

CHAPTER 2

THE CONCEPT OF LEARNING

Learning to pass examinations with distinctions demands a lot more than simply picking up a textbook, trying to understand what you are reading and then trying to commit it all to memory. In order to get outstanding results, your learning process must consist of a set of well defined and interrelated stages and activities. This is called the Concept of Learning.

LEARNING SHOULD BEGIN ON DAY 1

Many students begin studying only on the eve of their examinations. This should not be the case at all.

If you are guilty of the same practice, the first thing you have to do is to change your idea about what learning for examinations is all about.

Learning does not begin one or two months before the big day. It should start on day one of the course you are taking. If you are sitting for a school examination or an external examination, preparation should begin on the very first day of school for that academic year. Your state of preparedness should not end till you finish your last paper!

THE
3 STAGES
OF LEARNING

Altogether, learning is made up of three stages which form the structure and backbone of this entire book. They are outlined below.

Mastering Learning Techniques

STAGE **1**

Here, I will share with you breakthrough accelerated learning techniques such as Mind Mapping®, which was invented by Tony Buzan, and "supermemory" to help you study more efficiently and effectively.

The Journey To Success

STAGE **2**

The focus here is on how you can consistently build yourself up for the examination. You will learn about the power of goal setting. We will also deal with that nasty habit, procrastination, and how to motivate yourself to take action. In addition, you will be acquainted with the art of consistency and how you can make time work for you. Finally, you will learn to enhance your resourcefulness to achieve your outcomes.

Examination Skills

STAGE **3**

At this stage, you will learn how to build yourself up to being in peak examination condition and perform well under intense examination pressures. Taking an examination is in itself an art. Mastering this art can make all the difference – between scoring an 'A' or a 'B'.

WHAT IS LIMITING YOU NOW AND WHAT DO YOU WANT INSTEAD?

Before you go on reading, you must have a good idea of what you want to achieve at the end. When you know what you want, you will begin to read with a sense of purpose and this in turn would allow your subconscious mind to search for the answers to your quest, and to answer any questions you may have along the way.

YOUR MOVE!

The first step to knowing what you want is to take stock of what is limiting your success right now. No matter how well you are doing in school, I believe that there are limiting strategies that you want to change, so that you can do even better. Before you begin, you need to decide what these limiting strategies are and be fully aware of them.

Write down all the reasons you can think of as to why you are not getting the results you want. Two examples are provided.

1. Poor memory
2. Lack of motivation
3.
4.
5.
6.
7.

Now that you are aware of what you must rid yourself of, list all the skills or abilities you believe you will need in order to get the results you truly desire. Two examples are provided.

1. Time management skills
2. Effective note-taking skills
3.
4.
5.
6.
7.

As you read this book and learn the tools I share with you, I want you to:

CROSS OUT EACH OF YOUR LIMITATIONS as you become free of them.

and

TICK EACH SKILL AND ABILITY NECESSARY FOR SUCCESS as you begin to acquire them.

By the time you get to the last chapter, you will have acquired all the skills and abilities needed for success and be free of your limitations, forever! Now let us move on and discover more about the power of self-belief, one of the basic ingredients for success.

CHAPTER 3

THE POWER OF THOUGHT

'A' STUDENTS CAN BECAUSE THEY BELIEVE THEY CAN

Before you can learn and apply any technique or strategy successfully, it is very important for you say honestly whether you think you can become an 'A' student.

In fact, the way you have been answering this question to yourself has dictated your performance all along and the way you answer this question in the future will determine whether you will indeed become an 'A' student.

This may seem very simplistic to you but it is not. It is this perception you have of your ability that is dictating your every action, and your every attitude towards studies, and hence determining your results, good or bad.

I am not suggesting that merely by thinking that you are an 'A' student, you will become one. No way! To turn thoughts into reality, you need the skills and action.

However, if you do not even think you are capable of such an achievement, then you have already lost the game. You will not have given yourself the option of aspiring for 'A's.

Now, let me explain how powerful these beliefs of who you are and what you are capable of really are.

THE WAY YOU SEE YOURSELF... CAN MAKE OR BREAK YOU

The way you see yourself (your self-image), determines what you think you are capable of, and this in turn affects how much effort you will put in. Your efforts will, of course, affect the results you get and, ultimately, the results you get will reinforce your self-image.

WHAT IF YOU SEE YOURSELF AS HOPELESS AT STUDIES?

If all along, you have been perceiving yourself as 'hopeless at studies', then you are probably going to think to yourself that no matter how hard you study, you'll only get 'D's. So, you probably will not put in much effort and as a result, you spend little time on preparing for examinations, falling prey to other distractions like TV.

The end result would be just what you expected. You will score 'D's and even 'F's. This is what is called a self-fulfilling ('F' - 'F'ul'F'illing) prophecy.

Do you know what happens next? You will reinforce your negative self-image by saying to yourself, 'See, I knew I was hopeless!' and the whole cycle will repeat itself. I have many friends who are caught in this vicious cycle of failure and who cannot get out.

HOW TOP ACHIEVERS SEE THEMSELVES

Top students, by contrast, have very high self-esteem. They see themselves as 'A' scorers. In fact, they will not settle for anything less. As a result, they study with passion, utilizing their time efficiently and putting in more effort than anybody else! Finally when they get the 'A's they fully expect, it reinforces their positive self-image and boosts their self-esteem. These students are in what is called the Cycle of Success.

TIPS

Begin to see yourself as an 'A' student. Act the way you would if you were an 'A' student and do the things these great students normally do. If you are not sure how, then pick a role model (a friend who is scoring excellent results) and model his or her everyday behaviours and strategies. If you can duplicate these strategies, then you can duplicate the results! Some of the things you can imitate are:

1. the beliefs they have about studying
2. the beliefs they have about what they are capable of doing
3. how they spend and manage their time
4. how they ask questions and make notes
5. anything else you can discover about them

THINK ABOUT IT!

What would you do, if you were an 'A' student?

THE WAY YOU THINK OTHERS SEE YOU

It is strange, but we often behave in a manner that conforms to how we think others see us. For example, I know students who really want to change for the better, but who do not. The reason is they seem reluctant to change because they are afraid that their friends may mock them. You, too, may have had friends who, when you make a positive effort to work hard, sarcastically say, 'Wow, you're so hardworking! What are you trying to prove?' When this happens, you may get embarrassed; you do not want to destroy your 'cool' image, so you revert to your old behavior.

Don't let peer pressure keep you from changing for the better. True friends will support whatever positive changes you make.

SELF-IMAGE =SELF IMPOSED BELIEFS=

Aren't the perceptions we have of ourselves true? What if I really was a loser, you may ask. Firstly, the image you have of yourself is just your belief. It is not necessarily an accurate reflection of what you truly are.

The beliefs you have accumulated about yourself, collectively becoming your self-image, are nothing but the result of generalizations you have made about your past actions.

HAS THIS HAPPENED TO YOU?

Perhaps when you took your first maths quiz, you failed badly. Chances are, if it happened just one more time you would have formed a belief that 'you are not good at maths'. This is a generalization of a past action and if you hold this belief about yourself, chances are, you will fail again, thereby reinforcing it over and over again until it becomes true.

The point is that you may not be bad at maths at all! Perhaps you did not understand the relevant concepts or use the techniques taught well enough to pass that test.

Perhaps you used the wrong strategies or misread the question. We all make mistakes now and then. But using the wrong techniques and believing that you are inherently bad at the subject are two very different things.

When you tell yourself that you used the wrong methods, it does not affect your self-image and therefore, your future results. However, if you start saying, 'I failed because I'm no good at...', then you change your self-image and, as a consequence, seal your fate.

YOU ARE MORE THAN JUST A LABEL

Throughout our lives we constantly make generalizations about ourselves, based on our actions. As a result, we collect a whole lot of labels which we then stick onto ourselves. Some of these labels are 'I'm no good at maths' or 'I'm lazy'.

Then, besides the labels we put on ourselves, there are those that others, such as our teachers, parents and friends, use to describe us. Over time, we forget that these labels are just inaccurate beliefs. We are so used to them that we treat them as realities that we live by. The quality of the life you are living right now is a direct result of the labels you have collected and pasted on yourself.

LESSONS ON LIFE

My 'bad at Maths' label

When I was about six, my parents tried to teach me the multiplication tables but I just could not understand what 'multiply' means and therefore, I could not remember the multiplication tables. My parents were frustrated and frequently commented, 'It's so simple. Other children your age can multiply so why can't you?'

Soon, their frustration rubbed off on me and dealt a big blow to my self-esteem. I began to associate maths with feelings of frustration and failure and started daydreaming in class. I didn't even attempt to do my homework. Not suprisingly, I failed maths repeatedly and before long, I believed that I was simply not a 'maths person.'

Yes! I had given myself a 'bad at maths' label and I carried this label all the way to Secondary One.

I would have been condemned for life had it not been for something that happened that changed my self-image forever.

One day, the teacher set us a quiz on mathematical functions and the night before, I had worked extra hard figuring out the concept. The next day, when the teacher asked a question, I was the only one who could give the correct answer and a clear explanation! The reason for my sudden spark of genius was simply that I was the only student who had bothered to read ahead.

My right answer and explanation amazed my teacher and classmates. Friends began asking me for help with their homework. People began to label me as being 'good at maths' and gradually I came to expect that of myself. I began to work hard to maintain my new image and started scoring 'A's consistently. Maths suddenly became fun.

Eventually, I went on to major in maths in junior college, scoring 'A's in both college maths and further maths. Once again, my beliefs had become reality. Such is the power of labelling.

But why wait until someone gives you a 'gifted' label? You can give it to yourself now!

THE POWER OF BELIEF

You have just learnt that the beliefs you have about who you are can make an incredible difference as to how you live your life. In general, the beliefs we have about anything around us will determine the quality of our lives.

If you believe that school is boring, then you will probably get average results. If instead, you believe that school and learning are fun and exciting, then you will probably get better grades. If you believe that Chinese is the most difficult language in the world, then you will probably never master it.

The important thing to note is that beliefs are never absolutely true, and are merely generalizations. But if we believe in them, they will indeed become true. This is the power of beliefs. Let me further illustrate this with a true-life instance.

LESSONS ON LIFE

The four-minute mile

For thousands of years, people believed that it was impossible for a human being to run the mile in less than four minutes but in 1954, Sir Roger Bannister overcame this supposed 'impossibility'. He broke this mental limit that men had set within their minds. The interesting thing is that until Roger Bannister accomplished this feat, nobody could run the mile within four minutes. Yet, within one year of Bannister's breaking the barrier at Oxford, thirty-seven other runners also broke it, and in the following year, another three hundred did the same.

Why? Because Bannister's achievement had destroyed people's limiting beliefs of what was possible. How did Bannister do it? Besides physical training, he had constantly reminded himself mentally that it was possible. He rehearsed the run mentally until, to him, it became attainable! There are hundreds of other similar stories that support the power of self-belief.

INSTALLING USEFUL BELIEFS

If believing in something can really make it come true, then why don't you throw away all the beliefs that have limited you in the past and begin to adopt more useful ones?

Instead of keeping labels that others have stuck on you, create your own positive labels. You may want to give yourself a label like 'I am a diligent person' or 'I am an excellent manager of time'. In the next exercise, you will practise doing just this.

YOUR MOVE!

STEP 1 Starting right now, write down, in the space on the next page, statements concerning your self-image. What kind of person do you think you are? What are some of the labels you have picked up over the years?

Most importantly, describe the kind of student you believe you are. Are you hard-working or lazy? Are you a slow or a fast learner? Take some time now to analyse yourself.

I believe I am....

1.
2.
3.
4.
5.

STEP 2

Now, examine all the negative beliefs you have formed about yourself, and then look for all the possible reasons for not believing they are true. Remember, nothing is absolutely true unless you believe it to be so. Fill in the three columns below. The first line is given as an example.

	Negative belief	The real reason is because..	Examples of positive beliefs not true
1.	My memory is bad.	I have not learnt memory techniques to train my memory.	I memorize the lyrics of songs easily.
2.			
3.			
4.			
5.			

STEP 3

Here, write down what it would cost you if you continued to hold these limiting beliefs about yourself. Would it mean failing your finals and not making it to university? Would this be a blow to your parents? I want you to feel that it is absolutely necessary to rid yourself of these beliefs, right now.

	Negative belief	What they will cost me
1.		
2.		
3.		
4.		
5.		

STEP 4

Lastly, write down the self-image you would like to have. What kind of beliefs about yourself would you need to have in order to get the results that you desire? Look for any past references to back up these new beliefs. If you look hard enough, you will be able to find them. An example is provided.

	New beliefs	References
1.	I am a motivated person.	When I was preparing to take my driving test, I spent three hours a day after school practising, even when I was exhausted.
2.		
3.		
4.		

NO REFERENCES?

CREATE THEM!

If you can't find any references to back up the belief you want to have about yourself, do what Roger Bannister did. He wanted to believe that he could run a mile under four minutes but he had no references to back up that belief as he himself never came close to achieving it. What was more, nobody in history had ever been able to do it.

So, what Bannister did was to create the references in his mind. He imagined himself accomplishing that 'impossible' feat, over and over again until, in his mind, failing was not possible. In the end, he materialized what his mind vividly visualized.

GET REAL?...*but it's the dreamers who are the achievers.*

Many people believe that by holding on to their limiting beliefs, they are just being realistic.

You must have heard friends or parents say, 'It's better not to be too ambitious. We must be realistic.' Most people who say this, or words to this effect, are fearful of challenges because they are fearful of failure. Such people lead limiting and boring lives.

Great people and super achievers are rarely 'realistic' or 'down to earth', at least not according to most ordinary people's way of thinking.

When the Wright brothers (inventors of the aeroplane), first conceived of the idea they they could invent a flying machine, people thought they were mad. Then, when adventurers first wrote about travelling to the moon, people called them crazy!

Take the example of Bill Clinton, the 'Comeback Kid' President of the USA, the son of a poor widow in a small farm state. When he had said that his ambition was to work towards becoming the President of the most powerful country in the world, his teachers, neighbours and relatives said, 'Get real, kid!' But like our greatest inventors, Clinton dared envisage the impossible in his mind and then steadfastly, despite many setbacks, worked on this dream until it became a reality.

You now see yourself as someone who is capable of anything. You have created labels for yourself that will empower you to take action. The next step is to adopt other useful beliefs that will help you to be successful in life and in school and the easiest way to do this is to duplicate successful beliefs. Just what are these? Read on to find out.

THE 5 BELIEFS OF SUCCESSFUL STUDENTS

1. FOR THINGS TO CHANGE, I MUST CHANGE FIRST.

It is useful to believe that you are responsible for whatever is happening in your life. If you are getting bad grades, if your teacher hates you or your parents treat you like a child, then you must have been responsible for their beliefs either by your actions or by your negative thoughts. By putting the responsibility on yourself, you are putting yourself in charge of your life. Since you created the situations, you can change them.

However, if you, like most other students believe that bad things just 'happen to you' and you blame everyone and everything for your failures, then you will become powerless to change the situation. This belief is not at all useful.

So, if you want your grades, or anything in your life, to improve, don't hope that your teacher will change, your parents will back down or the examination will miraculously become easier. Instead, you have to start by first changing your own actions and behaviour.

2. THERE IS NO FAILURE, ONLY FEEDBACK.

Successful students encounter failures too, but if and when they do, they regard failure as 'feedback'. These students treat mistakes or failures as an outcome which they can learn from and constantly change their study techniques or strategies until they succeed. Unlike other students, they do not allow failures to discourage them.

3. IF OTHERS CAN, SO CAN I!

Everyone of us basically has the same brain capacity or neurological make-up. So why do some of us perform exceptionally well while the rest turn in a mediocre performance? It's because the super performers have learned to *access* their brain power. This, coupled with their strong powers of concentration, produces the fantastic results you don't even dare fantasize about. But now, with the super learning strategies you are about to learn, you too can tap into your amazing brain and get the same results!

4. STUDYING IS PLAY.

Absurd notion? Well, think again! Top students enjoy their studies as much as their play. They know that before you can ever be good at anything, you must first love and enjoy it. In this book, you will learn study techniques that will remove the pain from learning and put the joy back into it.

5. FLEXIBILITY PUTS YOU IN CONTROL.

'You must unlearn what you have learned,' – Yoda to Luke Skywalker in Star Wars – The Empire Strikes Back.

Successful students know that success depends on flexibility. They are able to change their behaviour and strategies to reach their goals, knowing that those who are inflexible or unadaptable simply get left behind.

As we go on, I will teach you to use your brain in ways that you never have done before. You may even feel uncomfortable at first. This is because society has programmed you to follow certain rules that are not at all useful to learning or behaving. In order to break free from the rut you are in and scale to greater heights, you must unlearn what you have learnt, and be prepared to learn new things that will transform your life forever.

LESSONS ON LIFE

Change comes from within

Chris was an angry and frustrated sixteen-year-old who had a problem communicating with his parents. He felt they did not trust him and the restrictions they imposed on him were ridiculous.

Chris had to be home by seven on weekdays, and on weekends, he was only allowed to stay out until eleven-thirty at night. Most of his friends stayed out way past midnight on weekends, with no questions asked. His entreaties to his father to stop treating him like a child fell on deaf ears. In defiance, Chris would return home past his curfew hour each time, and for this he would be reprimanded by his angry father.

When Chris approached me for advice (after I had directed a few SuperTeen camps, I became an unofficial counsellor to troubled teens), the first thing I told him was that *he* was responsible his parents' mistrust of him. Chris was surprised but he listened carefully when I explained that if he wanted things to change, he would have to change his behaviour first. 'How?' he wanted to know and I gave him a few pointers.

So a changed Chris began returning home before his curfew expired. He also began cleaning his room without being reminded to. His mother was further pleasantly surprised when he began helping out in the kitchen. Then, one night, when he had planned to go out to the cinema, he told his surprised father, 'I think I'll stay home tonight. I've a class test tomorrow and I don't feel I've prepared enough for it.'

Guess what happened next? Well, his parents began changing the way they regarded him and that changed their behaviour towards him. They began to regard him as a mature and responsible young man and after a month gave him more freedom!

Change your attitude & behaviour and you will see how it changes others' attitude and behaviour towards you!

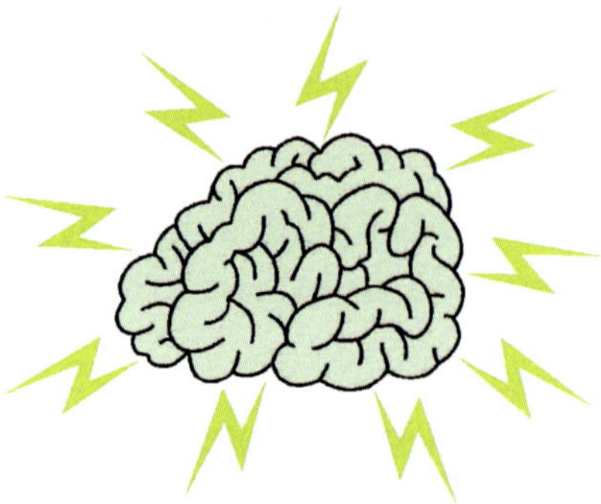

CHAPTER 4

YOUR POWERFUL BRAIN

A LOUSY BRAIN OR A POORLY UNDERSTOOD ONE?

You often hear people complaining that they are not as 'smart' as other people. They say they have a slower brain, a less creative brain or one that just cannot retain anything. In fact, many people believe that people are either born 'brainy' or not, if for whatever reason, they have been short-changed in the 'brains department' at birth, then they can never match up to someone else who was born more brainy, no matter how hard they study.

A MISSING INSTRUCTION MANUAL

Imagine this! One day you go out and buy the most sophisticated and powerful computer available, a million- dollar computer which can do virtually anything in seconds. You go home and try to execute a command for it to save. But each time you try, 'Error' flashes across the screen and you get frustrated.

What would you do? Blame the computer and say it's lousy? No, you probably woudn't do that because you spent a million dollars on it. So you believe that it must be able to save information once you can find the right command to do it.

You flip through the instruction manual and find that you had forgotten to key in a particular command. Sure enough, when you give the right command, the computer saves perfectly.

So how does this relate to our brain? Just because we did not pay a million dollars for it and were never given an instruction manual on how to use it, we often think it is no good when we cannot produce certain results, like remembering well.

Instead of trying to figure out the right 'commands' to 'access' our memory, we immediately give our memory a negative label. What does this do? It gives our brain an embedded command not to remember well in the future. We are, in fact, planting a virus in our brain!

THE BRAIN :

THE MOST POWERFUL COMPUTER IN THE WORLD

Are you astounded by the processing power of the latest personal computers on the market today? Have you ever wished that your brain could be as powerful as those computers? Well, did you know that the most powerful computer ever built, (a million-dollar supercomputer), is only equal in complexity to the brain of an ant?

Yes, and if a direct replica of the human brain could be built, it would equal, in terms of complexity and functions, a building 0.8 kilometres wide and 745.8 kilometres long. Furthermore, it would require a million and a half watts of electricity to run and nobody could afford to use it.

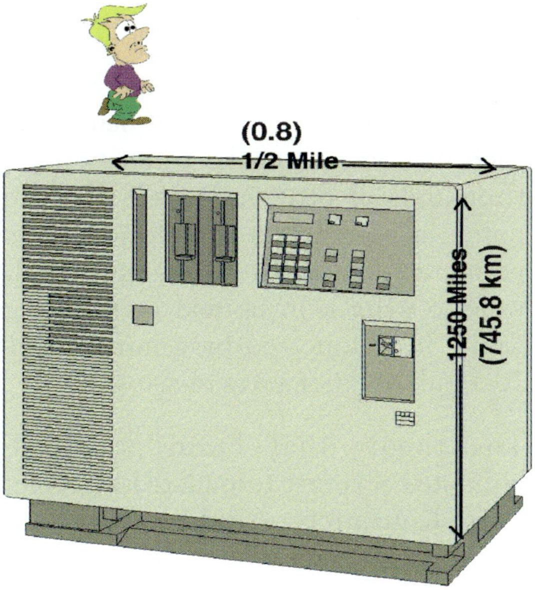

Astounding? Yet our brain weighs only 1.36 kilograms and runs on as much electricity as required by a ten watt light bulb. The brain is indeed the most powerful resource in the universe and its potential is unlimited!

The Brain's *Infinite* Capacity

'No human yet exists who can use all the potential of his brain. This is why we don't accept any pessimistic estimates on the limits of the brain. It is unlimited!'

– Professor Petr Kouzmich Anokhin

To understand why our brain's potential is unlimited, we need to know that based on existing research findings, the adult brain consists of approximately twelve to fifteen billion active nerve cells called neurones. Very early on after conception, each of our neurones makes connections with many other neurones creating neuroconnections.

Our brain power or intelligence is determined by two things, the number of neurones we have, but more so, on the richness of the connections. The more we stimulate our brain through exposure and learning, the more neuroconnections will be formed and the more intelligent we will become. The brain is therefore an elastic organ. The more we use it, the bigger and better it will get.

Your brain is like a muscle. Use it or lose it!

So what is the limit? What is the total potential capacity of our brain? Remember that we have 12 to 15 billion neurones and each neurone can make connections with thousands of other neurones. The total potential number of interconnections, if permutated, would be so large that if we were to write it in normal handwriting, it would be 1 followed by a mind-boggling 10.5 million kilometres of zeros!

The theory that brain potential is unlimited was first formulated by Professor Petr Kouzmich Anokhin who used advanced electron icroscopes and computers to come to this conclusion.

100000000000000000000000
000000000000000000000000
000000000000000000000000
000000000000000000000000
000000000000000000000000
000000000000000000000000
000000000000000000000000
000000000000000000000000
000000000000000000000000
00... *10.5 million kilometres long*

Infinite Brain Why *Finite* Results?

'It is not enough to have a good mind. The main thing is to use it well.'
– Rene Descartes

You are probably wondering why you are producing such terrible results if the brain is so fantastic and infinite in its potential. Why also do people have poor concentration and forget things so easily? The reason is because you have not learnt how to tap your brain's true potential. You have not learnt how to access the great memory or creativity that lies within. In fact, the most conservative estimate given is that we tend to use less than one percent of our brain's potential in our entire lifetime.

Your 2-*In*-1 *Brain*

To learn how to use more of your brain, you must first understand how it works. The top and central layers of the brain are made up of a left hemisphere and a right hemisphere. Connecting both sides is a network of nerve fibres known as the corpus collosum.

Each half has a different role. This discovery was made by Nobel prize winners Dr. Roger Sperry and Dr. Robert Ornstein of the California Institute Of Technology.

Our left brain deals with logic, linearity, analysis, language, sequence and mathematics. Our right brain takes care of things like rhythm, creativity, colours, imagination, holism and dimension.

Some people are right brain dominant while others are left brain dominant. Left brain people are those who are good at physics, mathematics and languages. Right brain people tend to favour painting, day-dreaming and listening to or creating music.

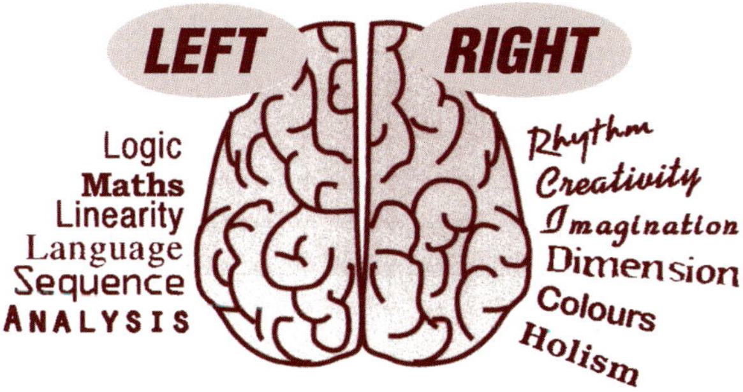

The Less Popular Right Brain

Both sides are equally important and powerful. They complement each other. Unfortunately society, and the educational systems created to serve them, emphasize left brain mental activities (like mathematics and logic) and pay attention to the right brain ones (like art and music).

Occupations emphasizing left brain skills like scientific research and engineering are valued more highly than right brain occupations such as those relating to art or music. This bias is built into our educational system right from the start. Have you noticed that out of all the subjects you have taken from the time you started school, only less than ten percent of subjects made use of your right brain?

This has two important implications!

1. Right-brain dominant students are almost doomed to fail academically as they are forced to learn and be tested using left-brain dominant methods. This makes demands on a hemisphere that has not been sufficiently nurtured. Are you one of these students? If so, prepare to turn your grades around as I teach you to use your right brain to study subjects associated with the left brain.

2. If all this while you have only used your left brain, what would happen if you were to start using both sides simultaneously in your learning? Wouldn't you double your brain power? Wouldn't you use more of your brain capacity?

So how do we learn to use both sides of the brain at the same time? Well, all the learning strategies that will be covered in the following chapters are based on this one principle of whole brain learning.

Most Geniuses Were 'Whole Brainers'

It has been found that men and women whom others have honoured as geniuses were merely people who could effectively use both sides of their brains. This gave them their extraordinary brain power.

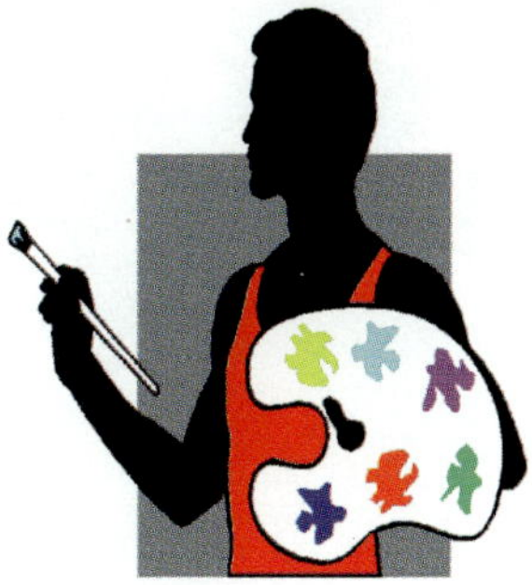

Leonardo da Vinci (1452–1519) who is honoured as one of the greatest artists of all times, was an accomplished mathematician as well. Did you know that he used mathematical formulas and theories to create the right balance of colours and artistic effects in his paintings?

Albert Einstein (1879–1955) used to fail mathematics at school and was considered a slow learner, but his musicality (a right brain trait), was well developed and he was both a credible violinist and artist. It was only when Einstein learned to use both sides of his brain that he unleashed his genius and formulated the Theory Of Relativity. He did it by first indulging in a right brain activity, day-dreaming. Einstein loved to day-dream, and one day, as he was sitting on a hill day-dreaming as usual, imagined himself riding a sunbeam to the far end of the universe, then returning towards the sun. That daydream suggested to him that the universe was in fact curved and hence space, time and light had to be, as well. This gave birth to the Theory Of Relativity. Other examples of whole-brain geniuses abound, if we but look for them.

CHAPTER 5

MIND MAPPING®

STUDYING WITHOUT THE PAIN

What if you could learn and acquire knowledge, i.e. achieve the results of studying, without all the pain frustration and boredom that comes with the process? Wouldn't studying then be fun and exciting and wouldn't you study more effectively and score better results? Yes, it is possible to eliminate all the pain associated with studying. In this chapter, we will learn to do just that! But first, you need to understand a few concepts associated with learning.

KEY WORDS

In your textbook, only the main points are important for the examination. All other information is less relevant. Now, even within the main points, not all the words are relevant. The relevant words are called key words and they carry the meaning of the main points. Examples of key words are nouns, adjectives and verbs, like 'boat', 'run' and 'letter'.

For example, in the chapter on 'Acids' in a Chemistry textbook, a main point may be: 'Acids have a pH reading of 0 to 7'. However, the entire meaning of that main point can be captured in just five key words. They are 'Acids' 'pH' and '0 to 7'. The other words like 'have a reading of' are irrelevant.

Roughly, in any paragraph of text, less than twenty percent of the words carry eighty percent of the meaning. This twenty percent constitutes the key words. Conversely, eighty percent of the words carry only twenty percent of the remaining meaning. These are the non key words.

The point is this. If we were to extract only the key words from our textbook, and study them, then we would learn just as effectively, but cut down our study material by more than one fifth! This means we can study five times as fast if we were to only study key words.

Not only that, with less material to study, we would surely remember better. Now you have understood what key words are and how they can help you, let's move on to:

IMPORTANCE OF NOTE-TAKING

If there is a golden rule to effective studying, it would be to make notes. Successful students always make their own notes. Unsuccessful students rarely make their own notes. They either study without notes or rely on their teachers to provide them with notes. So let's summarize the importance of taking notes.

1. It saves time as only main points are studied.
2. It aids memory as much less text needs to be covered.
3. It helps us study faster.
4. It cuts down the amount of study material, so studying is less overwhelming.
5. Revision can be done much faster.

CONVENTIONAL NOTE-TAKING

So with all the advantages of note-taking, are all the pains associated with studying eliminated? The answer is no. Studying is still, boring and the study material is still not organized in a way that allows for peak memory. The note-taking I am referring to is what most people are used to, i.e. conventional note-taking. Conventionally notes are made in linear form, i.e. they are written in sentences that flow from left to right, much like the way it is presented in the textbook, only now, the main points are highlighted.

FORMS OF CONVENTIONAL NOTES

FORM 1

There are two basic ways students or teachers make notes conventionally. The first type of conventional note-taking is made up of chunks taken out from the text. It is essentially identical to the original text, except that only the more important concepts are isolated. No effort is made to extract the key words and therefore, many redundant words are still found in such notes. Below is an example.

The Three States Of Matter

Matter has three states. They are solid, liquid and gas.

In solids, molecules are arranged closely, forming a regular pattern. Forces between them hold them in fixed positions. Because of the strong forces, individual molecules can only vibrate about their fixed positions.

In liquids, molecules are further apart and do not form any regular pattern. Forces between them are weaker and hence, the molecules are not fixed in positions. They can move among one another.

In gases, molecules are much further apart. They move at very high speeds and collide into one another.

FORM **2**

The second method is what is commonly known as writing in point form. Here, short sentences or phrases are numbered, with each sentence containing a relevant main point that needs to be learned. The sentences are normally arranged in a logical and hierarchical system to show how the concepts relate to each other. Many abbreviations are used and most of the words are key words. However, there may still be some non key words.

The Three States Of Matter

I. Solids

1. Molecules are arranged closely, forming a regular pattern.
2. Forces between the molecules hold them in position.
3. Molecules vibrate about their fixed position.

II. Liquids

1. Molecules are not arranged in a regular pattern and are farther apart.
2. Molecules are not held in fixed positions.
3. Molecules can move among one another. Hence liquids can flow.

III. Gas

1. Molecules are very far apart.
2. Molecules move at high speeds, colliding into one another.

CONVENTIONAL NOTES NOT GOOD ENOUGH!

Although the second method of note-taking is better, both forms of linear note-taking have their disadvantages and do not help us to reach our peak learning performance. The problems with these notes are as follows:

1. USE ONLY THE LEFT BRAIN

Linear notes contain only words arranged in a linear logical sequence (left brain function), i.e. there are no colours or images and creativity is not involved (right brain functions). They therefore do not promote whole brain learning.

2. CONTAIN NON KEY WORDS

Many non key words may still be included in the notes. They obscure the associations between key words and their inclusion makes revision a waste of time.

3. ARE DULL AND BORING

Conventional notes are made up of monotonous black and white words which make learning dull.

4. ARE NOT HOLISTIC

The notes do not allow you to see relationships or links between two or more concepts. This makes it more difficult for learning to take place as it does not allow a holistic view. In short, you cannot see the big picture.

5. DO NOT ALLOW IMPORTANT POINTS TO STAND OUT

No effort is made to make more important points stand out from the rest of the words. All words are in the same colour and are usually the same size. Although some students may use highlighters to make certain points conspicuous, there are better ways of making the material memorable.

MIND MAPPING®
WHOLE BRAIN NOTE-TAKING

Remember what we talked about earlier? If we can use both sides of our brains to study mostly left brain subjects, then we can substantially increase our brain power. This is also the principle behind a supermemory. You will learn more about how to do this in Chapter Six.

The question we pose here is whether there a technique of note-taking that not only eliminates monotony and boredom but also allows us to use our right brain to study left brain subjects? The answer is 'Yes'.

This form of note-taking, called Mind Mapping®, was first taught to me in the Super-Teen® programme by Master Trainer Ernest Wong. He was one of the first Asians to bring this technique to Asia, after being trained by the world renowned expert in 'learning how to learn' techniques, Tony Buzan.

ORIGIN & USE OF MIND MAPS®

Mind Maps® were invented by Tony Buzan and have been gaining worldwide popularity at a staggering rate. Mind Mapping® is a very powerful tool for brainstorming, creative thinking, problem solving, organizing of ideas and of course, note-taking. Mind Mapping® as a note-taking technique can be used for almost any subject and done in any language. It is especially useful for students in tertiary education and beyond, and this is because the more advanced the study material, the greater the need to condense and simplify it in a form that is easy to learn.

THE POWER OF MIND MAPPING®

Mind Mapping® is a way of making notes using colours and patterns, key words and images so that the information is rendered holistically.

When creating Mind Maps®, imagination and creativity are used to synthesize logically all the relevant key information in an organized way. Mind Mapping® taps your whole brain, releases your brain potential and improves your memory with less work. How exactly does Mind Mapping® help?

1.

IT SHOWS LINKS BETWEEN RELATED POINTS.

Unlike linear note-taking, Mind Mapping® allows you to link related concepts and points in a way that will help you to understand better. At one glance of your notes, you can see how all the ideas are related.

2.

IT 'JUICES' HEAVY STUDY MATERIAL.

Only key words are presented in a Mind Maps®, so they are thorough summaries of all the concepts and points that you need for a particular topic. Mind Mapping® will cut your study material by one fifth, reducing your study load. You will be less intimidated and overwhelmed by what you have to study. For example, an entire thirty-page chapter, which is normally summarized in several pages of laborious linear notes, can broken down into just one or two Mind Maps®. So which is more appealing and takes less time? Definitely Mind Maps®. Again,the fewer words to go through, the better your chances of recall.

3.

IT MAKES LEARNING FUN.

Unlike conventional notes, a Mind Map® is packed with colours, images, and other eye-catching creations left only to your imagination. Every single one of your Mind Maps® could be made to stand out in an interesting way. Looking at notes will never make you feel sleepy again, thus removing the drudgery associated with studying.

4.

IT FACILITATES THE DEVELOPMENT OF SUPERMEMORY.

Almost all the principles associated with supermemory are used in Mind Maps®. These include colours (colours increase your memory up to fifty percent), visual images, holism, creativity and imagination. Also, as only key words are used, ideas are linked together by these words, thus making them easier to remember.

5.

IT ENSURES DEEP UNDERSTANDING & RELEASES CREATIVITY.

Constructing Mind Maps® forces you to understand the topic thoroughly for it is only when you truly comprehend what you are reading that you can build a Mind Map®. You need to have a deep understanding of how the concepts relate to each other and exactly which concepts are relevant. You can then use your creativity, based on what you have understood, to create a Mind Map®. This is unlike conventional note-taking where you can blindly jot down points without really seeing connections between ideas. Therefore, when you make a Mind Map®, you have already won half the study battle.

MIND MAPPING® BASIC PRINCIPLES

Let's do a simple exercise that will give you an idea of what Mind Maps® are all about. In this exercise, you will make a Mind Map® of yourself. In the process, I will illustrate Mind Mapping® terms and concepts as well as introduce the laws of Mind Mapping®.

STEP 1

First, think of four things or more that you can associate with yourself. For example, if your name is John, see how many things can be linked with 'John'. Write all these four words, or preferably, draw images representing the meanings of these words in such a way that they are all attached to the image 'John'. A sample is given on the next page to guide you.

CONCEPTS TO ILLUSTRATE 'JOHN'

1. The image 'John' in the middle is called the central image. This is the main concept to which all other sub-points will be linked to.

2. The words and images attached to the centre are called first-level headings and they describe the central heading in greater detail. In this case, they are ' Family, 'School', 'Character' and 'Appearance.'

LAWS

1. The central image should be a multicoloured one that represents the entire topic being represented in a Mind Map®. It should not be enclosed within a border or a box. You may wish to supplement the image with words, if the topic is an abstract one.

Example:

LAWS

2. The first-level headings are key words and images that rest on thick, curved and organic branches. Notice that the line is attached to the centre. Notice also that any words used at this level must be in capital letters.

Example: 

3. In general, words or images in a Mind Map® rest on branches that are equal to them in length.

STEP 2

Next, write down or draw four (or more) words or images that can be associated with each first-level heading. The new words or images should describe the first-level headings in greater detail. See the sample shown on the next page.

A MIND MAP® OF MYSELF *WITH SECOND-LEVEL DETAILS*

CONCEPTS

These new words and images are called the second-level details. They provide details about the first-level headings to which they are attached. John's school has teachers, a building, offers subjects, and is located in the south. All these second-level details are attached to the first-level heading 'School'.

LAWS

1. The images or words used for the second-level details (and for all subsequent details e.g. third, fourth level etc.) must rest on curved branches of the same length. Note that unlike the lines of the first-level headings, these branches need not be thick.

2. Only key words and images are used in a Mind Map®. If key words are used, they should be printed clearly.

3. Branches are attached to one another. They should not be floating about.

Example: 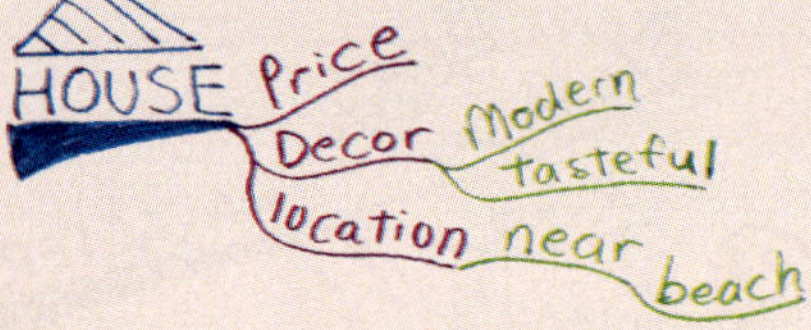

4. There should be only one image or word on one branch. Therefore, each image or word rests on an exclusive branch.

Example: 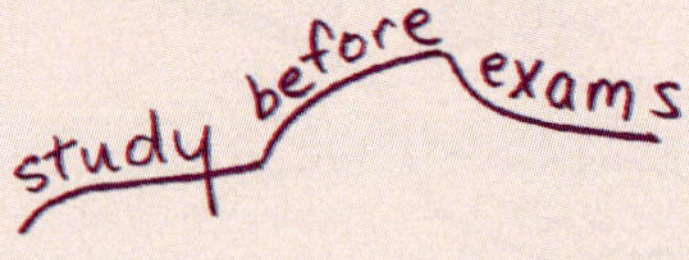

STEP 3

More images and words can be attached to these second-level details to describe them even further. These new images or words would obviously be called third-level details. For example, let's say the John's school was built in 1983, has many classrooms and is four storeys high and is white. All this new information can be attached to the second-level detail 'Building'. Of course, the other second-level details can be filled in a similar way.

A MIND MAP® OF MYSELF *WITH THIRD-LEVEL DETAILS*

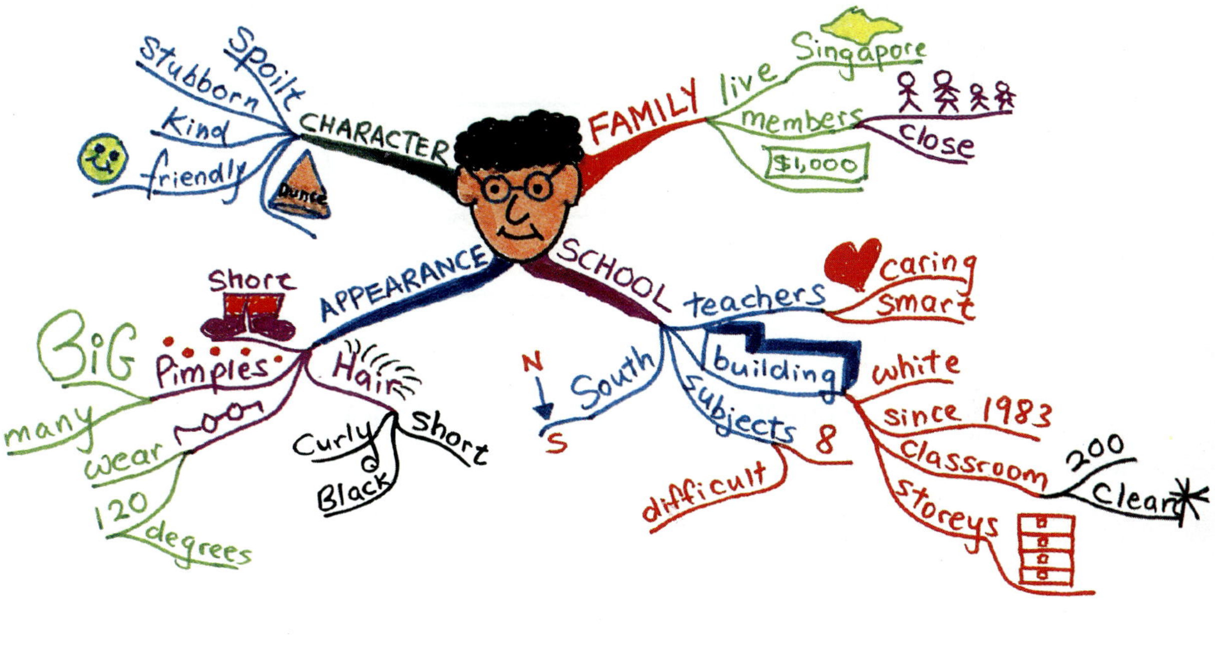

STEP 4

This process can go on and on as you branch out from each level into the next level with even greater detail.

MORE LAWS OF MIND MAPPING®

1.

DRAW ON HORIZONTALLY PLACED PAPER.

Your Mind Map® should be drawn on a piece of paper, the size of which is at least A4 placed horizontally. This is to allow room for the branches of the Mind Map® to radiate outward.

Example:

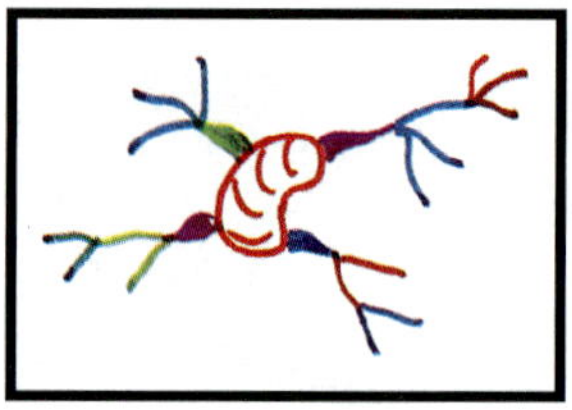

2.

COLOUR IN A PURPOSEFUL WAY.

Mind Maps® must be packed with colour to make them appealing to study. Also colour helps you remember better as it activates the right side of your brain. However, colours should be used properly.

Everytime you go from one level of heading or detail(e.g. second-level) to another one (e.g. third-level), you may want to make a change of colour. In other words, where a single branch splits up into many more, the new branches could be in a different colour from the primary branch.

Example:

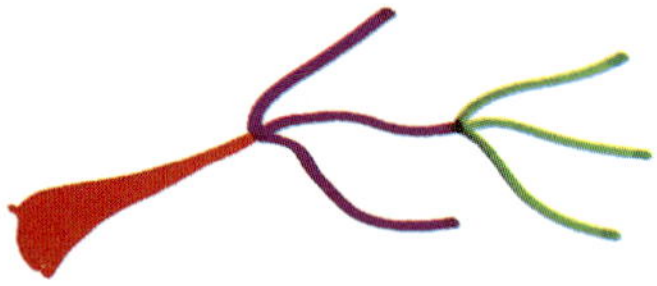

3.

USE ARROWS.

Arrows can be used to show relationships between two key words or images.

4.

PACK THE MIND MAP® WITH KEY IMAGES.

As far as possible, use images to convey the points to be studied. Images not only make the Mind Map® more interesting to study, but they also improve your memory. Remember, a picture is worth a thousand words.

5.

ABBREVIATE WHEN USING KEY WORDS.

Abbreviate key words, especially those that are always repeated. This will save you space and speed up the process. Go ahead and design creative abbreviations for yourself. Here are some I use regularly:

Key Word	Abbreviation
not whatever	~~whatever~~
without	w/o
because	∵
for	4
causes	⇛
through	
change	△
greater than	>

LINEAR NOTES V/S MIND MAPS®

Let's see how conventional linear note-taking compares with Mind Mapping®. The same topic of 'Matter' in 'O' Level Physics is expressed in the two forms.

Linear Note-Taking Method

The Three States Of Matter

I. Solids

1. Molecules are arranged closely, forming a regular pattern.
2. Forces between the molecules hold them in position.
3. Molecules vibrate about their fixed position.

II. Liquids

1. Molecules are not arranged in a regular pattern and are further apart.
2. Molecules are not held in a fixed position.
3. Molecules can move among one another; hence liquid can flow.

III. Gas

1. Molecules are very far apart.
2. Molecules move at high speeds, colliding into one another.

Mind Map® Method

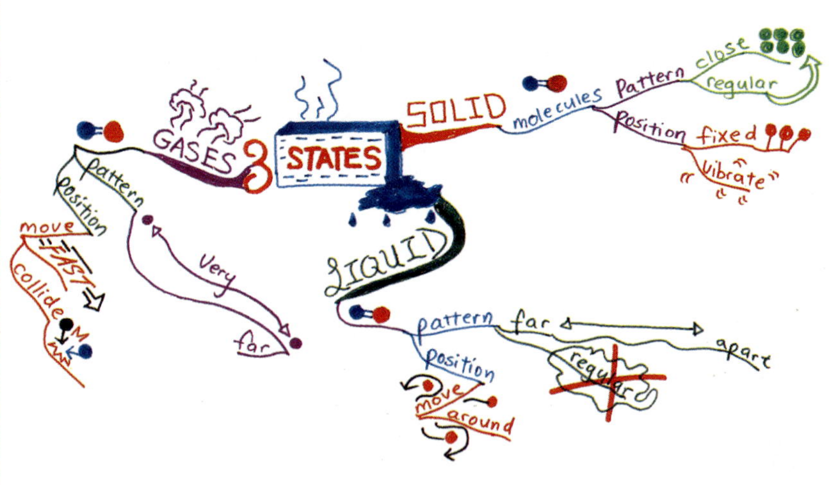

THE FLOW OF INFORMATION

Note that unlike all other forms of written communication, Mind Mapping® does not flow in a linear manner from left to right and downwards.

Instead, Mind Maps® are drawn, written and read starting from the centre and moving outwards and then in a clockwise* direction. Therefore, you will see that in the left-hand section of a Mind Map®, words are read from right to left (starting from the inside and moving outwards). The arrows positioned around the Mind Map® show the way the information should be read. The sequence of the numbers is another guide to the flow.

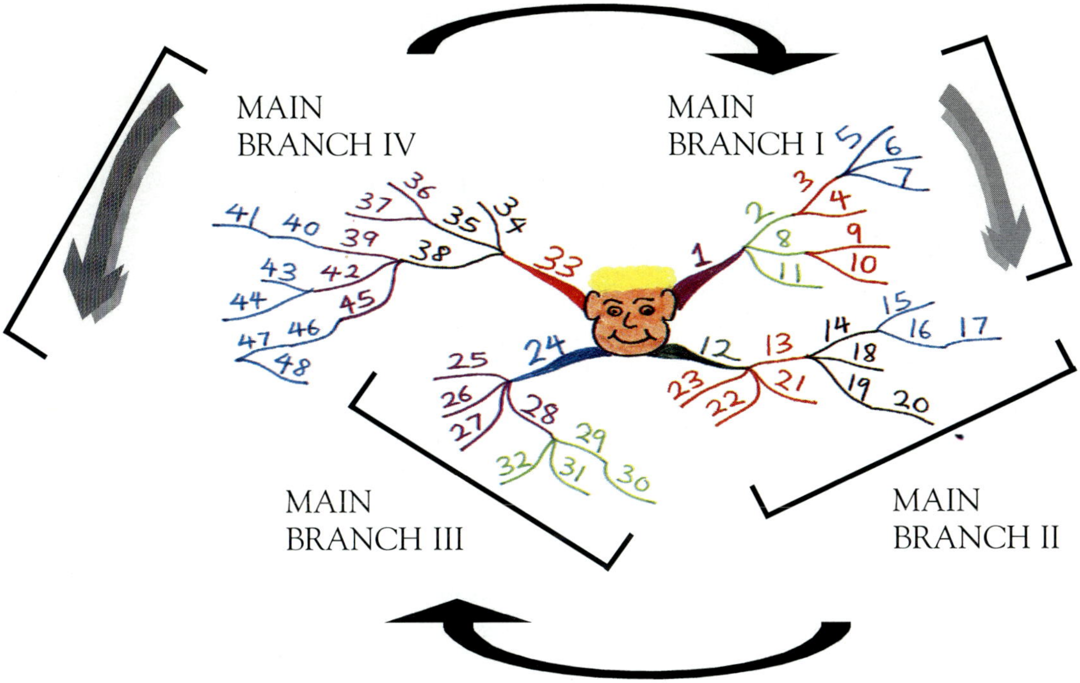

The four main structures labelled I, II, III, IV in the Mind Map® above, are called main branches. This Mind Map® has four main branches, because it has four first-level headings. The number of first-level headings always equals the number of main branches. Also, note that the main branches of the Mind Map® are read *clockwise, starting from Main Branch I to Main Branch II and finally to main branch IV. See the black arrows in the diagram. However, information is written and read from top down within each main branch. See the blue arrows in the diagram.

* Other Mind-Mappers® may choose to construct and read the main branches in an anti-clockwise direction or even in a random order. The choice is arbitrary.

THE MAKING OF...

A MIND MAP®

STEP BY STEP

Now, I will guide you through the process of making Mind Maps®, step by step. For the purpose of illustration, we will use an extract from a textbook to serve as an example, as we go through each step. This extract is from a Secondary school science guide, entitled *Excel In Science Secondary 1* (Oxford University Press). The material is taken from the Chapter 14, *Measuring Temperature*. This simple example was selected to make the illustration of the Mind Mapping® as easy to understand as possible.

Let's begin right now...

1.4 Measuring Temperature

What is Temperature?

1. The **temperature** of a substance tells us how hot or cold the substance is.
2. Temperature is measured with a **thermometer**.
3. The unit for temperature is the **degree celsius** (°C).
4. Sometimes the unit used for temperature is the **kelvin** (**K**).
5. Pure water boils at 100 °C and freezes at 0 °C under normal atmospheric pressure.
6. The temperature at which a substance boils is called its **boiling point**.
7. The temperature at which a substance melts is called its **melting point**.

Difference Between Temperature and Heat

1. **Temperature** tells us how hot or cold a substance is.
2. **Heat** is a form of energy which makes a substance hot.
3. Heat energy is measured in **joules** (**J**).
4. In the figure below, the water in beaker P contains twice as much heat as the water in beaker Q but both are equally hot as the readings on the thermometer show.

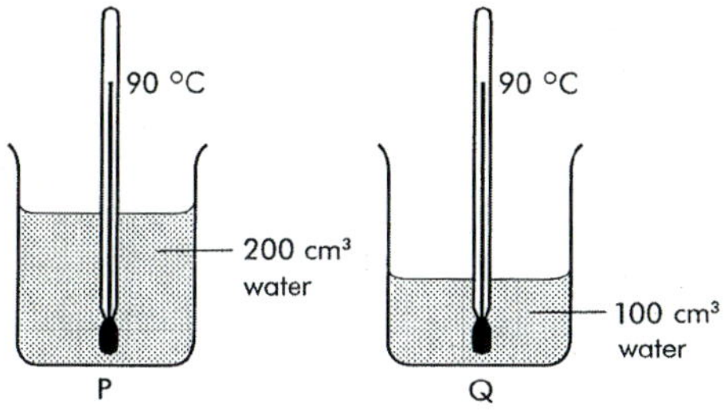

Water in beaker P contains more heat than water in beaker Q, but both are at the same temperature

Laboratory Thermometer

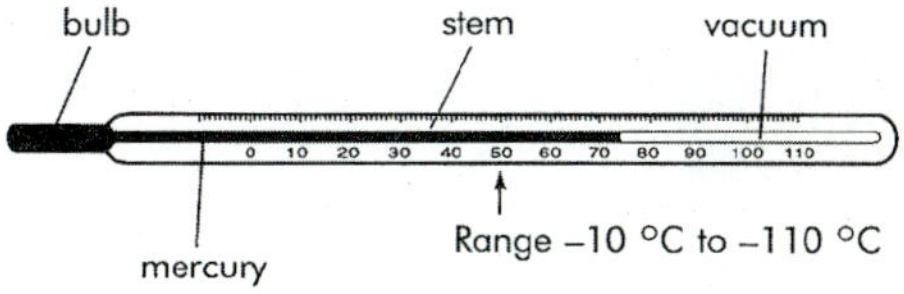

A laboratory thermometer

1. **Special features**:
   (a) usually measures temperature from –10 °C to 110 °C
   (b) has a long glass tube with a graduated narrow bore
   (c) has a thin-walled glass bulb containing mercury
   (d) has a vacuum in the space above the mercury
2. **How it works**:
   When the bulb of the thermometer is warmed, the mercury in it **expands** and rises into the long glass tube.
   When the bulb of the thermometer is cooled, the mercury in it **contracts** and falls down the tube.
3. **How to use the thermometer**:
   (a) Hold the thermometer by the glass tube. (**Never** hold it by the bulb.)
   (b) When taking a reading, the thermometer must be upright so that the meniscus is level with your eyes.
   (c) Read the top of the meniscus.
4. **Precautions to take**:
   (a) When reading the temperature of a liquid, do **not** take the thermometer out of the liquid.
   (b) Take the temperature reading only when the mercury has stopped rising or falling.

16

STEP 1

Read the subject matter thoroughly and pick out the main points. You can highlight the paragraphs to make them stand out. Next, underline the key words of these main points. Only these key words will be in your Mind Map®.

STEP 2

Plan how many Mind Maps® you will need in order to cover the entire chapter. One Mind Map® should contain one central image and should have about five first-level headings.

Depending on how long each chapter is, and how much relevant information is in it, different chapters will require different numbers of Mind Maps®. Some chapters may require only a single Mind Map® while others up to five. This is based very much on your judgement. Squeezing too much into one Mind Map® would make it very cramped and difficult to read. On the other hand, you don't want too many Mind Maps®, each giving very scanty information. The information given in the extracted text can be easily contained in a single Mind Map®.

STEP 3

Place the paper down horizontally. Next, draw a central image in the middle of the paper. If you are using only one Mind Map® for a chapter, the central image should be the title of the chapter. For example, if you are doing a Mind Map® on 'Hydrogen', then the central image should be 'Hydrogen'.

If instead, your chapter on 'Hydrogen' is made up of three Mind Maps®, then the central image of the first Mind Map® could be 'Hydrogen I', the second could be 'Hydrogen II' and the third, 'Hydrogen III'.

Solution: Draw an image to represent the title 'Measuring temperature'. Refer to diagram below.

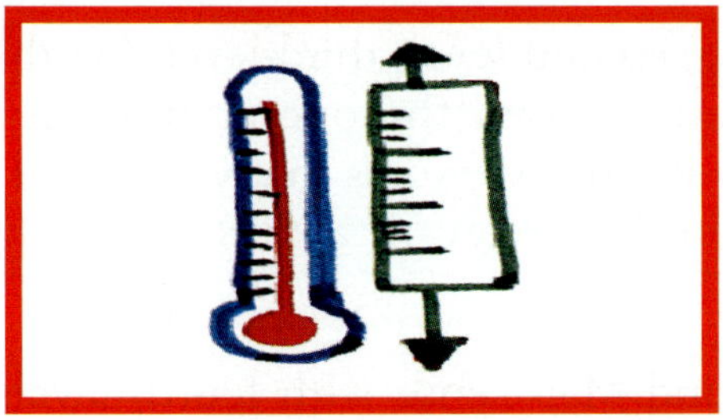

STEP **4**

Next, add the first-level headings around the central image. These first-level headings may at times be the sub-headings given in the chapter, but you can plan your own first-level headings, depending on your needs.

Solution: The first-level headings are 'What is temperature', 'Differences between temperature and heat' and 'Laboratory thermometer.'

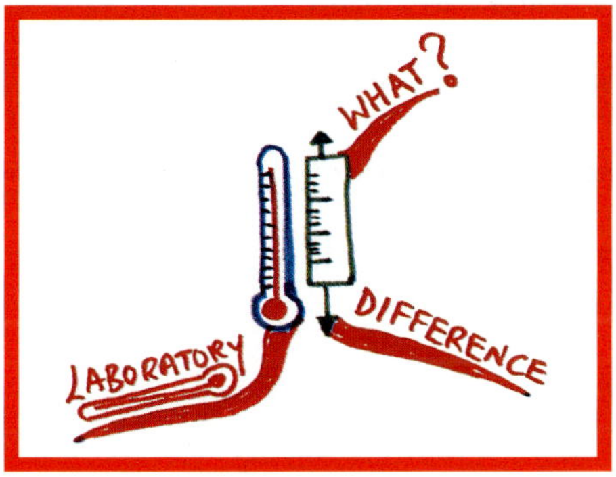

To recapitulate, the first-level headings should be:

1. key words and/or images

   Example: The key word 'What?' simply replaces the sub-heading 'What is temperature?' in the textbook.

   'Difference' represents the first-level heading 'Difference between temperature and heat'.

2. in capital letters if they are key words

3. resting on a thick, organic branch.

STEP 5

Next, we add details (e.g. second-level, third-level, fourth-level etc) to each of the first-level headings starting from the one at the top most right and moving clockwise. These details are the key words that you picked out earlier from the text. Continue this process until all relevant details of the chapter have been written down.

In our example, the Mind Map® ends with fourth-level details. However, Mind Maps® of subjects that secondary and junior college students take can have up to six levels of details.

Solution: Adding the second and third level details to the first first-level heading, we will get the diagram on the following page. On the next page, is the fully completed Mind Map® with details added to all the first-level headings.

To recapitulate:

1. only key words and images are used
2. only one word rests on one branch
3. branches are curved and connected
4. many colourful images are inserted, wherever appropriate

MEASURING TEMPERATURE MIND MAP® (WITH DETAILS ADDED TO THE FIRST FIRST-LEVEL HEADING)

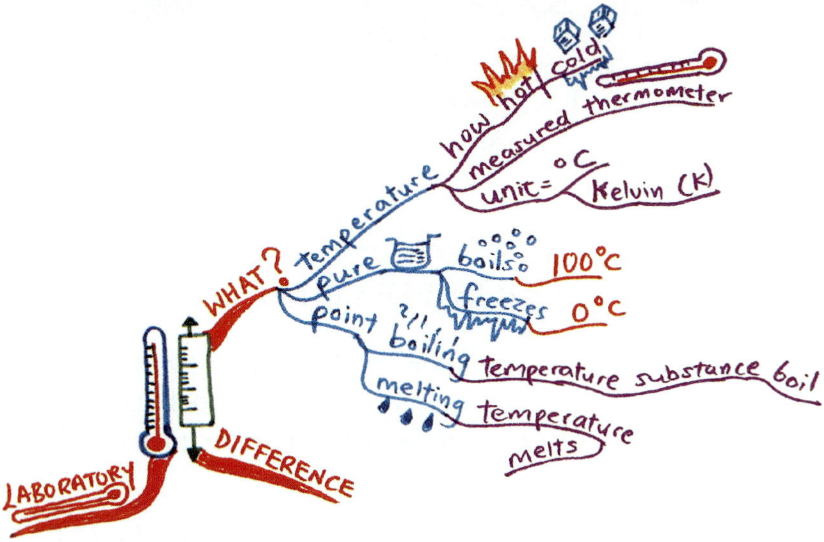

MEASURING TEMPERATURE MIND MAP® (COMPLETED)

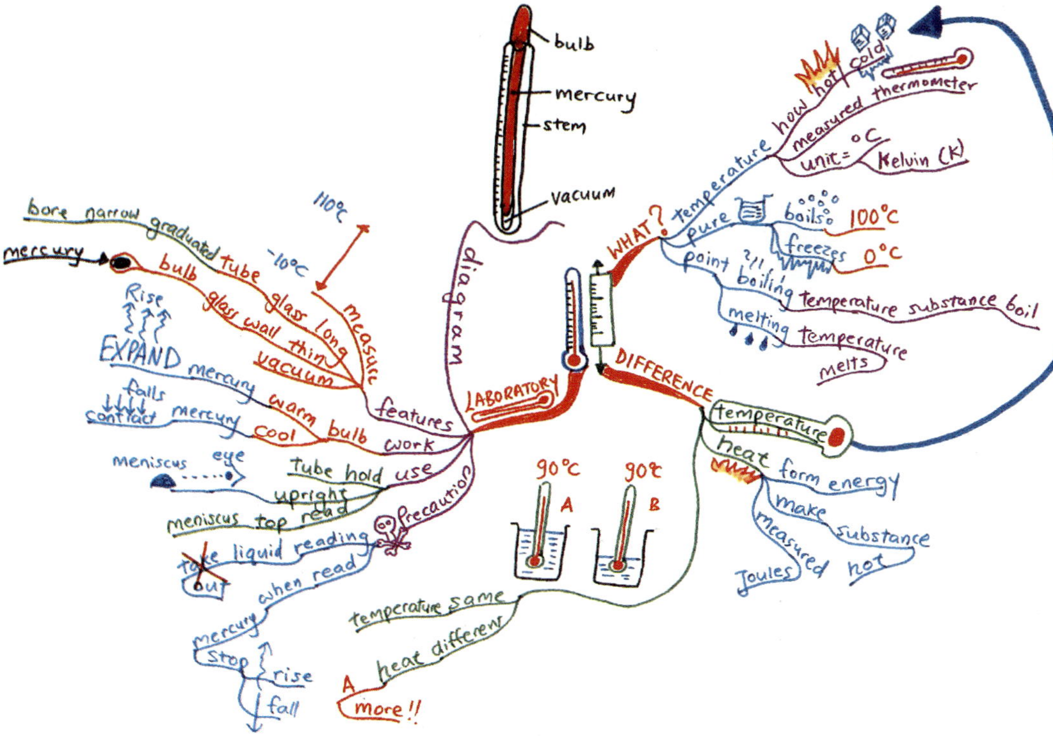

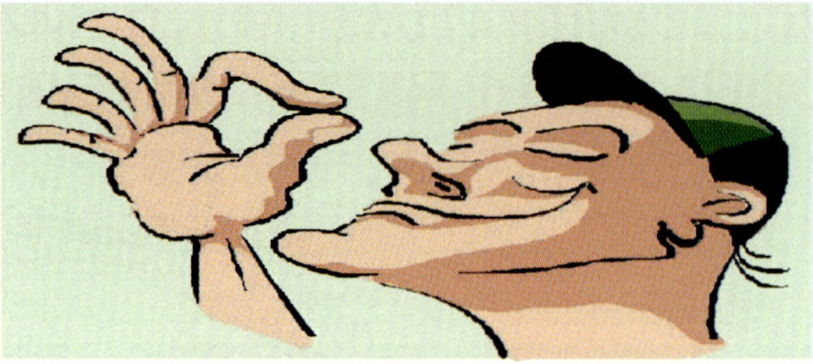

ARE YOU READY TO DRAW YOUR FIRST MIND MAP®?

At this stage, you should be well versed on how to create a Mind Map®, so get ready to do just that. First, read an extract from a Geography book *Excel in Geography for Secondary 1* given in the next three pages and as you do so, pick out the main points and key words. You can use a highlighter to do this.

Next, prepare the following materials you will need for your Mind Map®.

1

One to two pages of blank paper of at least A4 size. Art paper is excellent for drawing Mind Maps®.

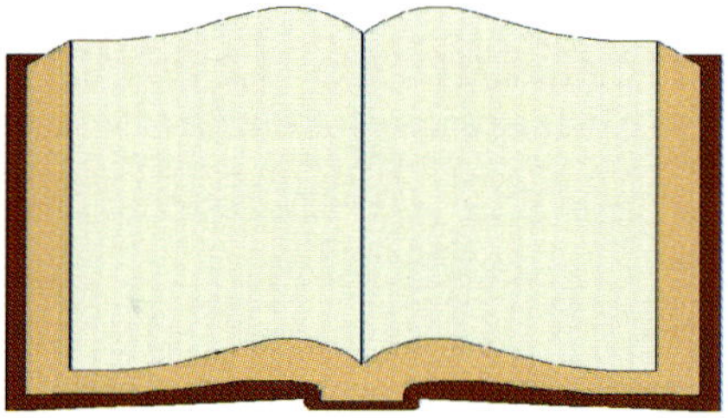

2

A set of colour pens or markers. Be sure to get those with fine tips.

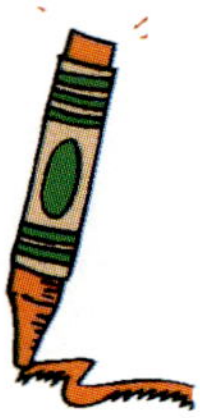

Great! You can draw your Mind Map® of the extracted text material on page 56. When you have finished the sample, check the Mind Map® on page 57 but remember, there is no one correct way of creating a Mind Map®.

This concludes the chapter on Mind Maps®. In the next chapter, you will learn how to remember the information you have included in your Mind Maps®.

EXTRACT

7 ROCKS AND LANDFORMS

Rock Types

There are numerous types of rocks that differ in their colour, appearance, texture, structure, hardness, composition, permeability, degree of resistance to denudation, and other physical and chemical characteristics. The three main type of rocks are igneous rocks, sedimentary rocks and metamorphic rocks.

Igneous Rocks

1. Igneous rocks are formed by the cooling and solidification of molten rocks such as magma and lava within the earth's crust or when they reach the surface.

2. There are two main types of igneous rocks:

   a. plutonic or intrusive rocks which have cooled slowly at great depths of the earth's crust. Granite is the most common of the plutonic rocks

   b. volcanic or extrusive rocks which are formed by the cooling and solidification of lava after a volcanic eruption. The best known volcanic rocks are basalt.

EXTRACT

EXTRACT

Sedimentary Rocks

1. Sedimentary rocks are derived or secondary rocks formed from the deposition and accumulation of materials on land surface or underwater (in lakes, seas and oceans) after millions of years.

2. The sediment and rock fragments that eventually form sedimentary rocks are brought about by the various agents of denudation and deposition. They are washed off by rain, rivers or waves, caused to slide down mountain slopes by frost and snow, dragged away by glaciers or blown into the air by winds and storms.

3. Thick layers of sediment become deeply buried, compacted or cemented into layers of rock strata, undergoing gradual and physical and chemical changes. Sedimentary rocks are thus also known as stratified rocks. Subsequent earth movement such as folding and faulting may lift these sedimentary layers to greater heights. The sedimentary rocks found up the Himalayan Ranges are believed to be from the seas and Indian Ocean and lifted during the Alpine earth movement some 35 million years ago.

4. Sedimentary rocks are thus looser and less consolidated than either igneous rocks or metamorphic rocks. Due to their nature of formation in areas with many living creations, they often contain fossils.

5. Successive deposits of various sediment in land and on sea eventually form various forms of sedimentary rocks, e.g. gravel becomes conglomerate, sand forms sandstone, clay is compacted into shale and lime emerges as limestone.

EXTRACT

EXTRACT

Metamorphic Rocks

1. No one has actually seen the process of the formation of metamorphic rocks, as this occurs deep within the earth's crust, mostly in a semi-molten state and under superheated conditions. All metamorphic rocks were originally igneous or sedimentary rocks and have become changed in both their appearance and character. They exist in a large number of varieties and are often of much greater value than their original rock type.

3. The metamorphosis (i.e. the process of change) of these rocks may have resulted from any of the following:

    a. heat, which causes the mineral constituents to re-crystalise, e.g. at more than 2000°C

    b. stress, which brings about the alteration in the rock structure, e.g. during folding and faulting

    c. pressure: at depths of 50 kilometres below the surface of the earth so that unstable minerals in rocks undergo chemical adjustment to form new rocks

    d. water, which dissolves some rocks and deposits other minerals

4. Metamorphic rocks are changed rocks with new chemical and physical properties, quite different from their original rock type. Many have a banded structure, with wavy bands. They can be fine or coarse-grained.

5. Metamorphic rocks, having undergone metamorphism or change becomes more valuable. For example, shale is changed to slate and schist, sandstone into quartzite and limestone into marble.

EXTRACT

YOUR MIND MAP®

Draw your Mind Map® placing paper horizontally.

MIND MAP® ON 'ROCKS AND LANDFORMS'

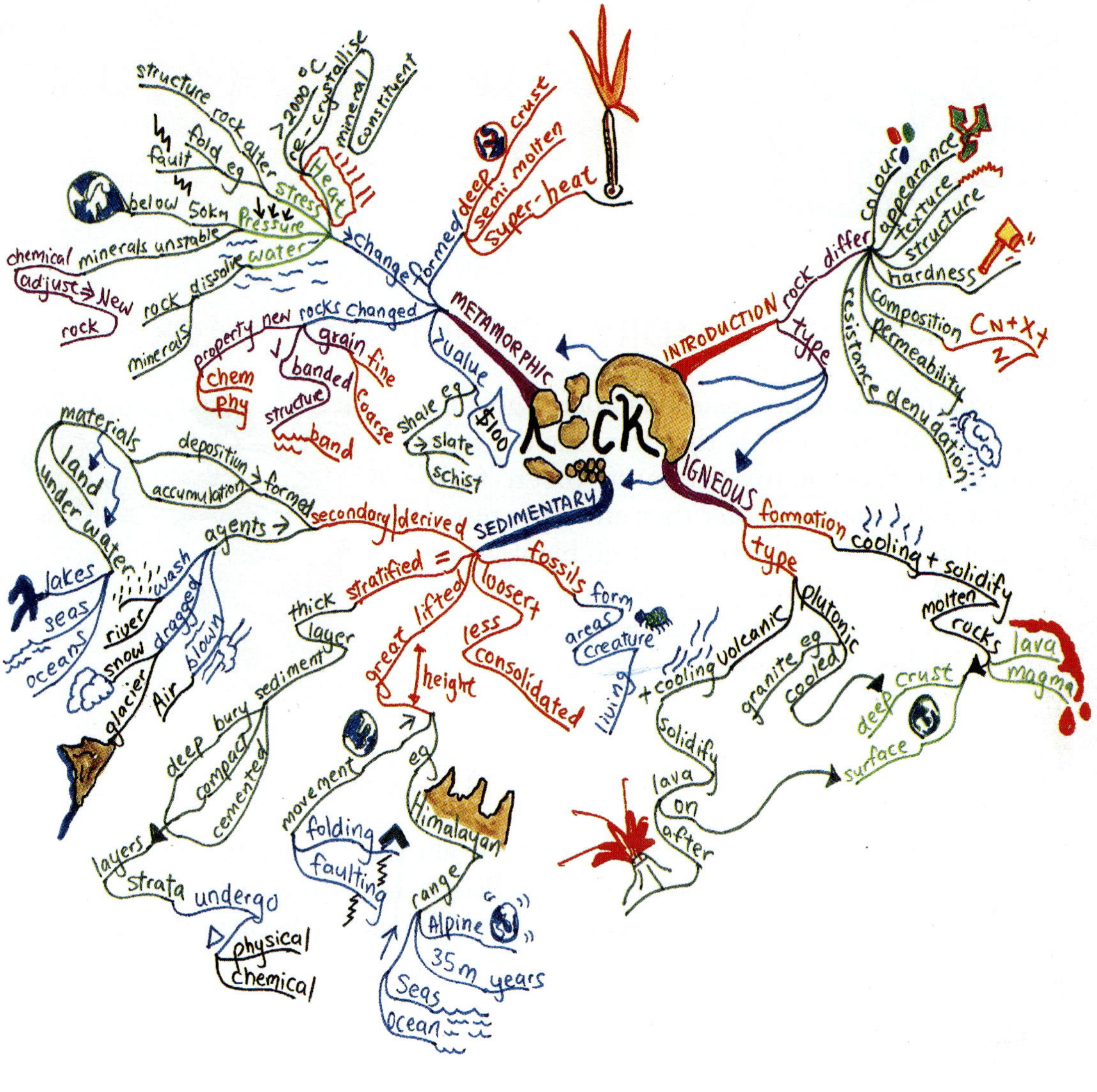

CHAPTER 6

SUPERMEMORY FOR WORDS

IS YOUR MEMORY HOLDING YOU BACK?

One of the most common reasons students give for not doing well in school is that they have a poor memory. In fact, many students often fully understand the subject matter they are being tested on completely, but their minds just go blank when they have to produce an answer in the examination. As a result, their grades do not reflect their true ability in the subject being tested.

THE GIFT OF MEMORY

Many students have the misconception that the ability to remember well is a gift or a talent that some have and others do not. People who think they do not have a good memory give up trying to remember things completely because they expect to forget them. Sure enough, having a poor memory becomes an excuse for failing and they will continue to produce bad results.

YOU CAN LEARN ABOUT SUPERMEMORY, TOO!

The first thing you have to understand is that there is no such thing as a good or bad memory. There is however a difference between a trained memory and an untrained one. Studies have shown that people who had an extraordinary capacity to remember things, a fact often mentioned by memory expert, Harry Lorayne, did not have brains different from ours. Rather, they knew the correct keys to tap and so accessed their natural memory.

So, remember, memory is not a gift. We already have a natural supermemory, which we only need to learn to access. Before you learn just how to do that, let's explore the notions of 'retention' and 'recall'.

PERFECT RETENTION *IMPERFECT* RECALL

The process of memory includes retention, registration and recall. Retention involves storing information which we are exposed to. 'Recall' refers to the ability to retrieve that information after it has been registered.

There is now increasing evidence to show that our ability to retain information is perfect and does not deteriorate over time. This means every word, picture or sound you have ever registered in your mind, since the time you were born, lies perfectly intact somewhere in your brain. The only problem is that most of the time we have problems recalling or retrieving the information.

A LIBRARY METAPHOR

So, if we can retain everything, then why can't we recall it just as effectively? To understand this, you must know that your mind is like a massive library which contains a huge amount of information in hundreds of thousands of books.

If I were to ask you to look for a particular library book, you would be able to do it easily by using the library's index system of arrangement, as the books would be classified according to details such as subject matter and author's name. But imagine, if all the books were haphazardly placed and no index system was maintained, it could take you months to find the particular book. Well, your ability to recall works in the same way.

Most of the time, the information we have consciously and subconsciously been taking in has not been stored in an orderly way for retrieval. Therefore, we find that we cannot recall it easily, although it is there. So, one of the keys to developing supermemory is to develop a well arranged index system in our minds. The way to do this is by using memory systems which will help you retrieve information quickly during examinations.

All memory involves linking one piece of information to another. More specifically, remembering anything new involves linking that piece of information to something we already know.

For most people who have not been trained in memory techniques, this linking process is a purely subconscious one. Sometimes our subconscious mind makes strong links and sometimes weak ones. When the links are strong, we find that we can remember the information easily. What makes the links strong are the principles of memory.

THE
PRINCIPLES OF MEMORY

You can probably cite me a hundred and one instances of you having forgotten something that happened very recently, like what you had for breakfast this morning. Yet, you also remember some things that happened many years ago, which you have not forgotten, and probably never will. It fact, you probably remember these experiences vividly, with all the associated pictures, feelings and sounds. One or two of these might have been traumatic or particularly memorable, such as an aeroplane trip or a first date.

What factors were present during these unforgettable experiences that allowed you to remember them? What principles allowed you to create strong links between the new information and the knowledge you already have? If you can identify what these principles are, you can apply them all the time so that you can have a good and reliable memory. Here are some of the most important ones:

Visualization

Our mind thinks in pictures. We therefore tend to remember pictures more easily than words. The more detailed and vivid the picture in our minds, the stronger our memory of it will be.

Association

We are also likely remember things associated with things we already know. Association forms the links between ideas we talked about earlier. This in turn creates an ordered index in our minds for quick recall. Linking pictures (visualization and association) in our minds is the basic principle behind supermemory.

Absurdity & Humour

We also tend to remember things that are ridiculous, funny and out of the ordinary. Ordinary things that occur in our everyday life are easily forgotten. It is often the outstanding, absurd and humorous events that create lasting memory. For example, if you were to see a bear drinking beer in a pub, do you think you will ever forget the astonishing sight?

Emotion

We also remember events that arouse strong emotions of fear, anger, love, pain and hate. You will probably always remember the time when you first fell in love!

Synesthesia

Involving all our five senses of sound, sight, smell, touch and taste, will greatly enhance our memory. This is because the use of all five senses creates an experience that is as close to reality as possible. You will learn how to utilize your senses in the memory systems.

Colour

The use of colour both in our imagination and in notes can increase our memory by up to eighty percent.

Meaning

We tend to remember things which we understand, and have meaning for us, rather than things that we try to memorize without actually understanding them.

Rhythm

Rhythm increases our ability to remember because it activates our right brain, a hemisphere usually dormant during study. For example, have you ever wondered how effortless learning the words of a song are compared to memorizing the same number of words in a history textbook? Ask yourself how you first learned the alphabet. Wasn't it through rhythm and rhyme in the 'Alphabet Song'?

MOVEMENT

The ability to visualize movement will also aid memory. The faster the movement and action, the deeper your impression will be.

REPETITION
REPETITION
REPETITION

Obviously our memory gets stronger as the material we are exposed to is repeated more frequently.

RELAXATION

Studies have shown that when the brain is relaxed (particularly exhibiting alpha brain waves), it can retain information much faster and better than when the brain is at the active beta level, i.e. under stress.

THE PRIMACY & RECENCY EFFECT

Studies have shown that we tend to remember things at the beginning of a study period (known as the primary effect) and things at the end of a study period (known as the recency effect). We will discuss this principle in greater detail in the chapter, 'Revision and the Pattern of Memory'.

MEMORY SYSTEMS

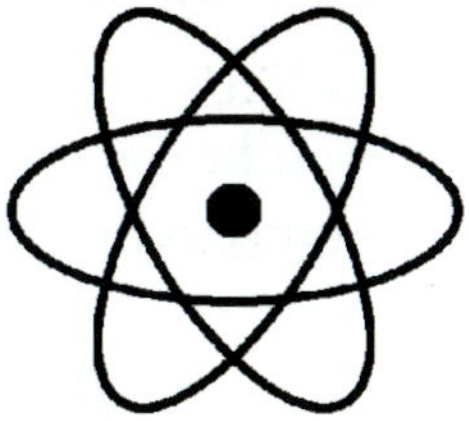

Memory sytems are techniques that will enable you to create strong links between new information that you want to remember and information that you already know. The process by which this is done is through the use of the principles of memory. The two most common systems are the Link System and the Number System.

THE LINK SYSTEM

What Is It Used For? It is used to remember a list of words or facts and it is especially useful for studying subjects with a lot of hard facts such as in physics, history, literature and geography.

The Process The Link System involves the use of your imagination to associate visual images of the (key) facts you would like to remember. You will, in the process, use colour, movement, absurdity and humour and all the other principles of memory. Therefore, the Link System involves two step: visualizing and association.

1 VISUALIZE

The first step is to create a picture of the words or objects you want to remember. For each word or fact, assign a detailed and vivid visual image. For example, if one of the words you want to remember is 'car', then see in your mind's eye, the picture of a car in detail. See the colour, shape, model, design and all the specific features. If you have a list of ten words you need to remember, create ten mental images in your mind.

2 ASSOCIATE

The next step is to link all the ten pictures together to form a story. It is very important to make these associations strong. The way to do this is to use all principles of memory in creating the story. In your story, there should be a lot of movement, many colours, music and rhythm and, most importantly, the story has to be ridiculous, funny and memorable.

A SIMPLE EXAMPLE: REMEMBERING A SHOPPING LIST

Now let's take a very simple example of how you can use the Link System to remember a shopping list of fourteen items. Imagine that your shopping list comprises the following:

1. egg	7. glasses
2. beef	8. orange juice
3. fork & spoon	9. soap
4. bikini	10. toothbrush
5. perfume	11. paint
6. banana	12. nail polish

Using the Link System, visualize yourself holding a smooth, hot **egg** as you leave your house. As you feel the smoothness, you make a hole in the shell. Out of this hole pops a cow's head (reminds you of **beef** steak) with two horns. The left horn is in the shape of a silver **spoon** while the right is in the form of a **fork**. You accidentally wave the fork which jabs a girl in a polka dotted **bikini** reeking of strong, sweet smelling **perfume** sprayed all over her. The pain makes her drop a long, yellow **banana** she is holding on the floor.

Not looking, you trip on the banana and go crashing into a row of crystal **glasses** filled to the brim with **orange juice**. The entire floor is dirty and the manager orders you to clean it up with **soap** but using only a **toothbrush**. However, as you the floor, you accidentally scrape off the **red paint**. Later, you cover up the paint scratches with red **nail polish**.

If you had used your mind to visualize the events that were described, you should remember the shopping list easily. In the space below, jot down as many items as you can remember. Now you have a go!

1.
2.
3.
4.
5.
6.
7.
8.
9.
10.
11.
12.

How many items could you recall? You may have missed one or two, but I'm sure that you managed to recall much more than you normally would have been able to. If you couldn't remember an item, it is probably because you did not create the image clearly in your mind's eye while listening to the story.

Notice that in creating the story that linked all the words, we used:

1. movement ('drop the banana', 'out pops a cow's head'),
2. humour ('jabs the girl'),
3. absurdity ('cow's horns in the shape of a fork and a spoon'),
4. sense impressions ('strong-smelling perfume'; 'hot smooth egg')

Again, it is very important that you use these memory principles to create strong links between the images. If you find that you cannot remember, it is because the links you created did not have sufficient movement, absurdity, humour or sense impressions.

IMAGING ABSTRACT WORDS

In most study materials, there will be many abstract words that you may find impossible to visualize. Under these circumstances, you must convert the abstract word into a visual image through the process of **imaging**. Only then can you use the Link System to associate the words. There are two methods, the Similar Sound Technique and the Trigger Technique.

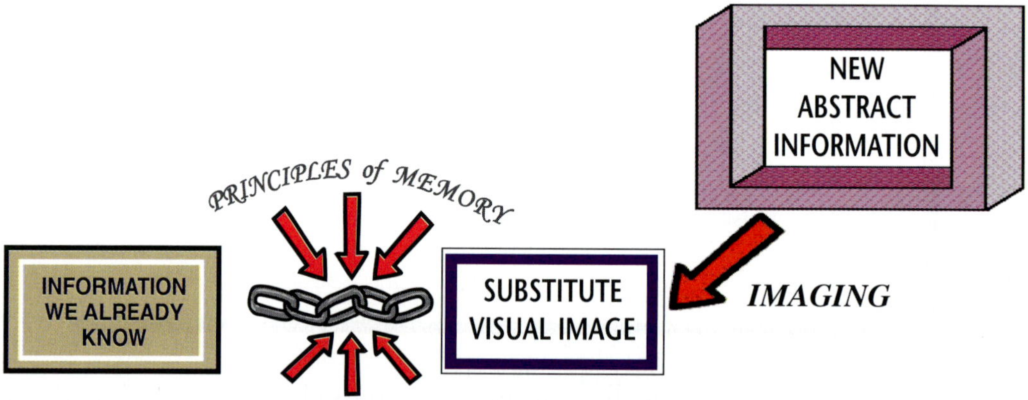

The Similar Sound Technique

To recall an abstract word, it must first be broken down into its syllables, and a substitute word or words which rhyme with the syllables of the abstract word are used instead. The substitute word(s) should be easy to visualize.

For example, the chemical compound chlorine is abstract, but it can be replaced by the word 'crawling' which rhymes with 'chlorine'. So, we can form a mental picture of a person crawling on the floor. When we think of the visual image, it would remind us of chlorine.

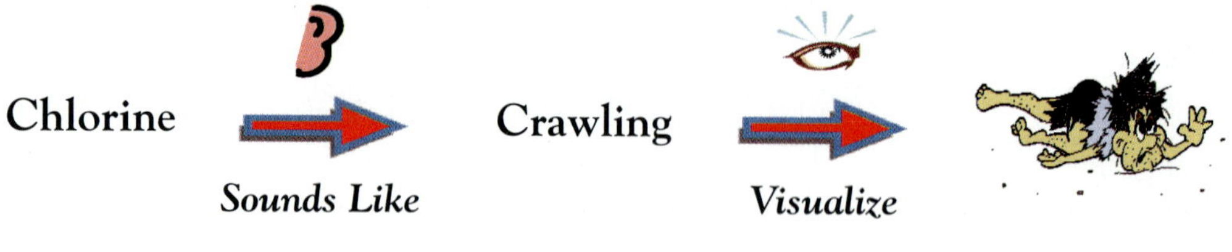

Next, think of the biological term 'colon', which means large intenstine. Since 'colon' sounds like 'cologne', simply visualize a bottle of cologne to remind you of 'colon'.

Lastly, think of 'photosynthesis'. What word sounds like 'photosynthesis'? The word can be broken down into four syllables: 'photo', 'syn', 'the' and 'sis'. 'Photo' reminds us of 'photograph'. 'Syn', 'the' and 'sis', combined, sound like 'seen the sister'. To remember, you can visualize a stranger coming up to you and showing you a photograph of a girl, while he asks you if you have seen his sister.

Got the idea? Good. Now, come up with at least one substitute word that sounds like each of the five abstract words listed below. Again, your substitute word must be easy to visualize.

Abstract Word	**Your Substitute Word**
1. gravity	
2. fluorine (chemical)	
3. glucose	
4. hydrogen	
5. oesophagus	

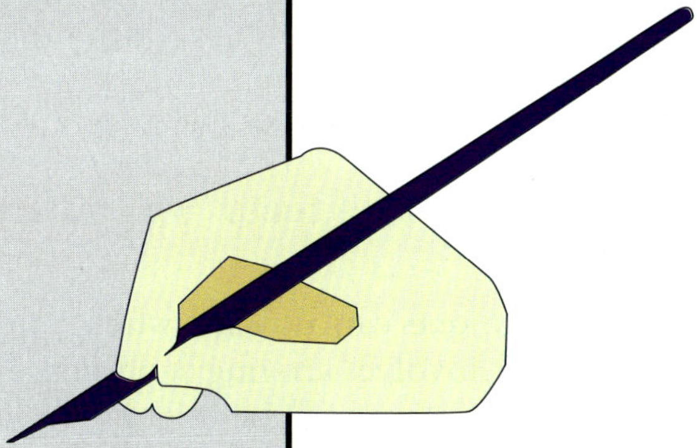

Possible Substitute Words

1. 'gravity' sounds like 'gravy' & 'tea'
2. 'fluorine' sounds like 'flower urine'
3. 'glucose' sounds like 'glue' & 'ghost'
4. 'hydrogen' sounds like 'high Trojan' (horse)
5. 'oesophagus' sounds like 'Esso for gas'

If you are studying subjects like history, literature and geography, there is rarely a need to use substitute words because most of the facts are tangible and easy to visualize. The only time you may need to substitute a word is when you have to remember names and places. The idea is similar to that demonstrated in the next example.

For example, say you need to remember that Napoleon was defeated in the Battle of Waterloo. 'Napoleon' (a name) can be broken up into the syllables 'nap', 'pole' and 'lean'. So, you could visualize Napoleon as someone who took a nap on a pole that was very lean. 'Waterloo' (a place), and when the word is broken up into syllables, it sounds like 'water' and 'loo'. To remember, you could visualize a loo (toilet) submerged in water.

To remember that Napoleon was defeated in the Battle of Waterloo, simply link the two images together using an absurd story. You could imagine the man taking a nap on a lean pole when he was shot down and fell into a loo (toilet) that was submerged in water.

THE TRIGGER TECHNIQUE

This technique can be used when you cannot find a substitute rhyming word. Basically it involves arriving at an image that leaps into your mind when you think of the abstract word. This is highly subjective and different people may see different things, but be consistent. Once you have chosen an image to represent a word, stick to it.

For example, what first comes to your mind when you think of the word 'economics'? You may think of 'money' or associate the word with 'offices' or 'people at work' and so on. The more specific the image the better. Visualizing money may not be very good because 'money' is very general concept. A good image to represent 'economics' is your economics lecturer's face.

How about 'oxygenated blood'? Again, you could imagine each small red blood cell wearing an oxygen mask.

What about 'population'? Does it remind you of many new born babies, crowded places and people of different nationalities? Again, use whatever image first comes to mind.

APPLYING THE LINK SYSTEM

Now, let's explore some examples of how the Link System can be used to memorize the facts presented below.

Subject 1: Elementry Physics

For this first example, let us consider something very simple. Let's say you want to learn the desirable features of an effective thermometer.

An effective thermometer is:

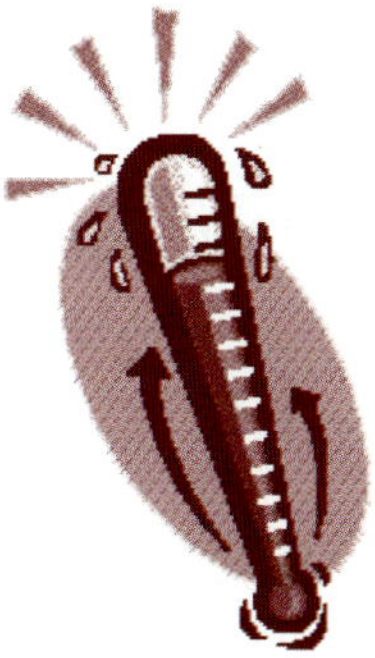

1. *easy* to *read*
2. *safe* to use
3. *inexpensive*
4. *sensitive* to temperature changes
5. has a *big range* of temperatures

1 IDENTIFY KEY WORDS

The first thing we need to do is to identify the key word or words in each of the five features listed above. Remember, not all the words are important and need to be memorized. We only have to remember one or two key words that will give us the entire meaning of each feature. The key words are highlighted on the previous page.

2 VISUALIZE

The next step is to create a visual image for 'thermometer' (the main subject we are learning about) and for each of the five features listed above. Remember, if the features are abstract, we have to use either the Similar Sound Techinique or the Trigger Technique to create a visual image for them.

The first thing we need to visualize is the main subject, thermometer. See in your mind's eye a gigantic, glass thermometer with a bulb of mercury at one end and tiny black markings over the length of its body.

Now, let us form images for all the five features. The first feature is 'easy to read'. So you could visualize someone reading a thick blue book (remember to add colour) very quickly, flicking the pages to and fro (remember to have a lot of movement).

Triggers

EASY to READ → READING A BOOK QUICKLY

The next key word is 'safe'. Since you cannot see the word 'safe' (in this context, it means 'protected from danger'), we will use the Similar Sound Technique. Notice that it sounds like 'safe' (meaning a security vault). Therefore, to remember 'safe', we visualize a large, black, metal safe with a combination lock on it.

SOUNDS LIKE

SAFE (protected from danger) → SAFE (vault)

For the next key word, 'inexpensive', we can use the Trigger Technique (ask yourself what is the first image that comes to mind) to create a visual image that represents it. In this case, perhaps you could imagine a bag of one-cent coins to represent 'inexpensive'.

Triggers

INEXPENSIVE → **BAG of ONE CENT COINS**

The next key word is 'sensitive'. Again, using the Trigger Technique, we can picture someone crying because he or she is very hypersensitive.

Triggers

SENSITIVE → **SOMEONE CRYING**

As for the last set of key words, 'big range', we can use the Similar Sound Technique to visualize a shooting range with many big targets.

Sounds Like

BIG RANGE → **BIG (Shooting) RANGE**

3

ASSOCIATE

Now that we have created a visual image for each point, we can link them all up using a nonsensical story with a lot of movement, humour, colour and other principles of memory.

I suggest you picture a gigantic glass thermometer with a bulb of mercury at one end and markings on its body. This thermometer is reading a thick blue book, flipping through the pages very quickly (reminds you of 'easy to read'). To his suprise, he finds a black, metal safe with a combination lock (reminds you of 'safe to use') between the pages of the book. Getting very excited, he opens the safe, only to find a bag of one-cent coins (remember 'inexpensive').

Disappointed, the thermometer starts crying (remember 'sensitive to changes in temperature') the tears dripping down its long body. To cheer himself up, he decides to go to the shooting range and shoot at the biggest targets (remember 'big range of temperatures'). See the story in the mind's eye and test yourself! Recall the five points discussed in this section.

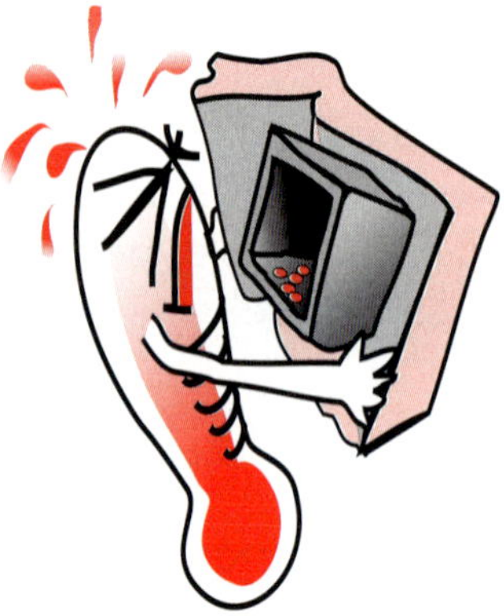

So what makes for a effective thermometer?

4

TEST YOUR MEMORY

Subject 2: Elementary Biology

Suppose you need to remember the functions of arteries (red blood vessels). The functions of arteries are as follows:

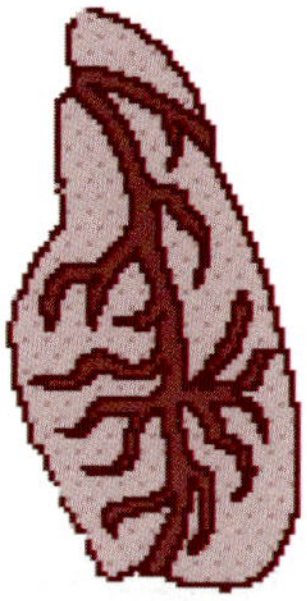

1. They have thick muscular walls.
2. They carry blood away from the heart.
3. They have no valves.
4. They carry oxygenated blood.
5. The blood they carry has very high pressure, and flows very fast.

1

FIND THE KEY WORDS & VISUALIZE THEM

Remember that you only need to select between one and three key words that would remind you of each entire point. You only need to create a visual image to represent those key words.

First, form an image of the word 'arteries'. You could imagine 'King Arthur' (sounds like 'arteries') sitting on a big white horse.

The first point is 'thick and muscular walls'. Note that 'thick' and 'muscular' are key words that are sufficient to remind you of that entire point. To remember them, visualize a very muscular man with very thick arms.

For point two, you only need to create a visual image for the words 'carry blood away heart'. Just imagine a man carrying a pack of blood and running away from a big gigantic heart that is thumping in the background.

For point three, the key words are 'no valves'. A valve is a type of device which works by opening and shutting. So just imagine that the object has many holes or openings around it which are blocked by stoppers.

The next point is 'red oxygenated blood'. You could see each individual blood cell as a tiny person wearing a red oxygen mask.

The last point describes the blood as being of 'high pressure and flowing very fast'. Thus the key words are 'high pressure' and 'very fast'. So visualize a person sweating, because he is under a lot of pressure, while running very fast.

2

ASSOCIATE

Now that we have an image for each point, we simply use an absurd, colourful, imaginative story with a lot of movement, to link all the words together.

Visualize King Arthur ('arteries') riding his horse and coming across a half-naked muscular man with thick arms ('thick muscular walls'). In his hands is a bag of red, viscous blood and he is running away from a big heart that is thumping in the background ('carries blood away from the heart'). Arthur knows that the man stole the blood and proceeds to stop him. He uses his sword to prise out the stoppers from the openings ('has no valves') causing blood to ooze out. Each blood droplet is wearing an oxygen mask. ('contains red oxygenated blood'). Meanwhile, the man is so frightened he sweats profusely and makes a speedy getaway ('the blood has very high pressure and flows very fast').

3

TEST YOUR MEMORY

Now write the answers based on having heard and visualized the story.

The functions of arteries are:

1. ______________________
2. ______________________
3. ______________________
4. ______________________
5. ______________________

Subject 3: Basic Economics

This is a popular pre-university or college course, so let's spend some time on the next section. Suppose you have to remember all the factors that influence the quantity demanded for a commodity. These factors are:

1. price of the commodity
2. prices of related commodities (substitutes)
3. taste and preferences
4. income distribution
5. population size

To remember these factors, imagine 'quantity demanded' as a child demanding sweets from his mother. To please the child, mother goes to the shop and finds the price of the sweets ('price of the commodity') too high.

So, she buys a similar type of sweets ('price of related commodities'). The child tastes it and likes it even more than the original ('taste and preferences'). In fact, he's so excited he spills a bottle of ink on the carpet, and the stain distributes ('income distribution' sounds like 'ink' and 'distribution') throughout the fabric. As the ink comes into contact with the fabric, it creates a loud 'pop'(sounds like 'population') sound which reverberates everywhere. Create the images in your mind's eye and test yourself when you are done.

With practice, you will find the link system a very powerful aid in studying. It impresses the facts very strongly in your memory and, as a result, allows you to retain information much faster. Instead of having to commit facts to memory using repetition, this system requires you to go through the facts only once. It also makes learning a lot more enjoyable and interesting.

FURTHER APPLICATIONS OF THE LINK SYSTEM
LEARNING NEW WORDS & THEIR MEANINGS

This technique is especially helpful if you are learning a new language or studying a subject that requires you to learn the definitions of many complex words.

The Idea Use the Similar Sound Technique to find substitute word(s) which sound like the abstract word you are studying. The substitute word(s) should be easily visualized. You then use a story to link the visual image of the substitute word(s) to the true meaning of the abstract word.

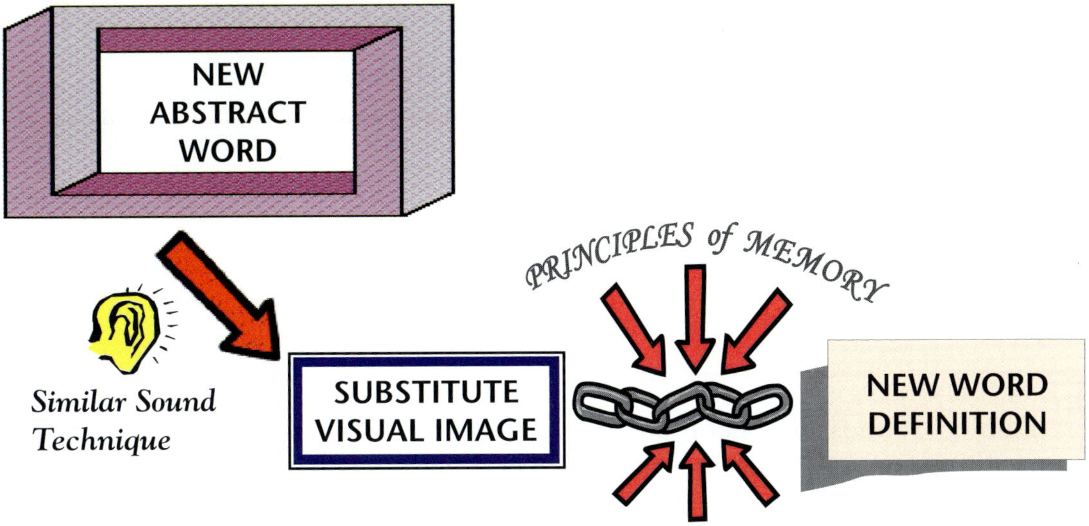

Some Examples Consider the following new words and their meanings which you may have to learn;

1. Poignant – A sharp pain

HOW TO DO IT!

First break down the abstract word into its syllables, if necessary. In this case, we get 'poig' and 'nant'. 'Poig' sounds like 'point' and 'nant' sounds like 'nun'. So imagine that a sharp point pierced a nun and caused a intense pain. So whenever you think of 'poignant', it reminds you of 'sharp pain'.

2. Exhort – To advise

HOW TO DO IT!

Again, break down the words into 'ex' and 'hort'. 'Ex' sounds like 'axe' and 'hort' sounds like 'hot'. Imagine that every time your father gives you advice, he holds a sharp axe with a hot blade threateningly, so you will heed him. When you are asked for the meaning of 'exhort', you will remember its meaning, i.e. to advise strongly.

3. Pumice – Volcanic stone

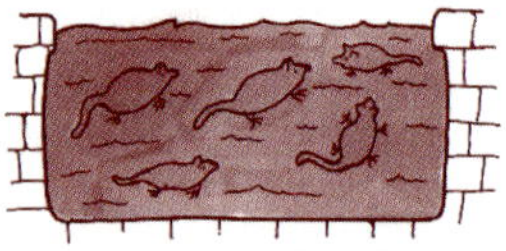

HOW TO DO IT!

'Pumice' sounds like 'pool' and 'mice'. To link the substitute word to the meaning, you could imagine the crater of a volcano filled with water (pool) and mice swimming in the pool.

4. Prodigy – Genius

HOW TO DO IT!

You can imagine a (pro)fessional who went (dig)ging for a special mineral which, when he ate, turned him into a genius!

5. Salient – Most prominent

HOW TO DO IT!

'Salient' sounds like 'sail' and 'ant'. Imagine an ant who excels in sailing and becomes the most prominent ant around. So when you think of 'salient', you will immediately think of 'prominent' (prominant).

6. Forebear – Ancestor

HOW TO DO IT!

Imagine that your ancestor was a circus trainer. His most famous act was training four bears (sounds like 'forebears') to play mixed doubles in tennis. Again, 'forebears' will remind you of 'ancestor'.

7. Amoeba – A one-celled organism

HOW TO DO IT!

Amoeba sounds like 'Amy' and 'baa' (the sound made by a sheep). You could imagine that a girl, Amy, suddenly starts to bleat ('baa') like a sheep because she is unable to speak like a normal person. Because of her strange behaviour, Amy has to be locked up in a prison with one cell! (a one-celled organism).

Go through all the material once, seeing the images in your mind. Then, write down the meaning of all the new words you have learnt.

TEST YOUR MEMORY!

Next to each of the words listed on the right, write down its meaning or definition.

New Word		Meaning
1.	poignant	____________
2.	exhort	____________
3.	pumice	____________
4.	prodigy	____________
5.	salient	____________
6.	forebears	____________
7.	amoeba	____________

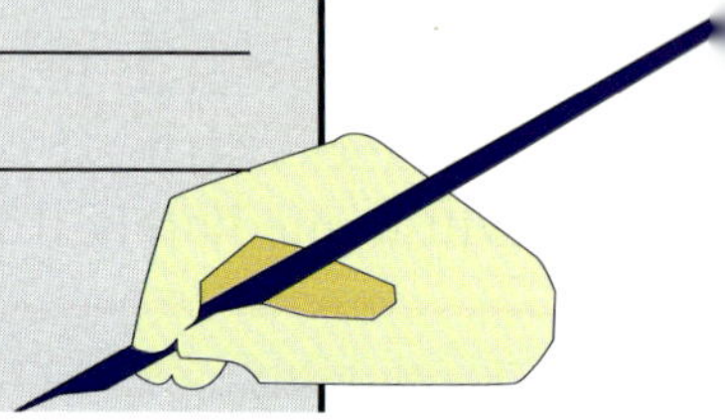

MORE EXAMPLES FOR YOU

Below are more new words you can practice with. Apply the same method and have fun doing it. Go through the words once, then visualize them as being part of ridiculous story. When you are done, test yourself and you'll be amazed at the results!

1.	emanate	–	to come or flow from
2.	monolith	–	a large block of stone
3.	equipoise	–	balance between competing forces
4.	herculean	–	very difficult
5.	mayhem	–	confusion
6.	mitochondria	–	a cell part that produces energy
7.	humerus	–	a bone in the arm

This concludes the chapter on developing an excellent memory for words. We will next look at how memory can be applied to numbers.

CHAPTER 7

SUPERMEMORY FOR NUMBERS

THE NUMBER SYSTEM

Unlike words, numbers are abstract. They cannot be visualized and hence associated with each other or with other items. The number system overcomes this obstacle by using phonetic sounds to assign a key visual image to represent each number. Once numbers can be visualized as images, they can be easily remembered. This technique is especially useful for remembering dates, formulae and chemical equations.

HOW IT WORKS

Every Number from 0 to 9 has got a phonetic sound associated with it. Once you have committed these sounds to memory, you can convert any number (even numbers with more than four digits) into a visual image which you can see in your mind and register in your memory. The ten basic numbers with their corresponding phonetic sounds are as follows:

Number	Phonetic Sound
1	d, t, th,
2	n
3	m
4	r
5	l
6	j, *soft* g, sh, ch
7	*hard* g, k, c
8	ph, f, v
9	b, p
0	z, ce, s

Notice that 1 has the sounds 'd', 't' and 'th' which sound similar. 8 generates the 'ph', 'v' and 'f' sounds. You can use any memory aid to remember these sounds, but let me share with you the most common methods used.

REMEMBERING THE PHONETIC SOUNDS

The number 1 is made up of a vertical downward stroke. Similarly, the letters 'd', 't' and 'th' are made up of that same one downward stroke.

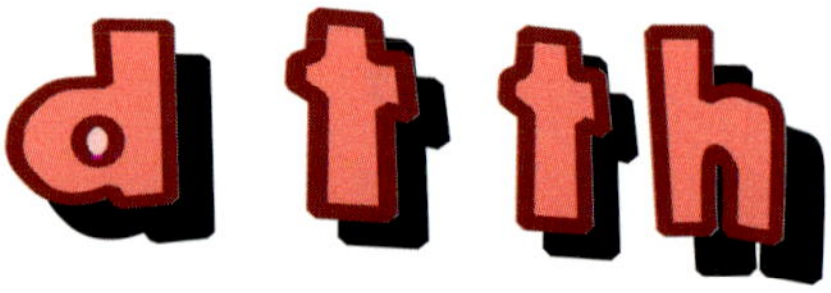

2 could remind you of the letter 'n' because 'n' has two downward strokes.

3 could remind you of 'm' because 'm' has 3 downward strokes. Alternatively, if you turn the number 3 ninety degrees in an anti-clockwise, you get 'm'.

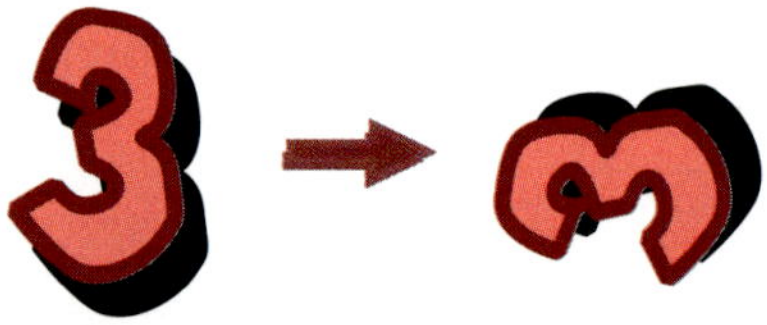

The number 4 is spelt 'four'. The last letter of 'four' is 'r'. Therefore, 4 will remind you of 'r'.

How about 5? Take a look at your right hand and your five fingers. Notice that the space between your index finger and your thumb forms an L shape. Thus, 5 will remind you of the letter 'l'.

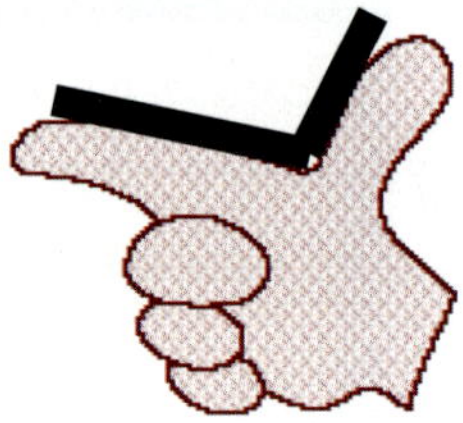

As, for 6, its mirror image looks like 'j'. The sound of j will remind you of the sounds of soft 'g', 'sh' and 'ch', or you could remember the phrase 'Jack cheats short giraffe'.

If you take the mirror image of 7 and look at it together with the original letter you will see the letter k facing downwards. Again, by remembering the phrase 'girl kicks cow', you will remember that the sounds *hard* 'g', 'k' and 'c' relate to 7.

If you look closely at the number 8, it looks like two 'f's facing one another. Therefore, 8 will remind you of f. Using the phrase, 'Philip fools vampire', you will remember that 8 reminds you of phonetic sounds 'ph', 'f' and 'v'.

9, when seen upside down, looks like a b while the mirror image of 9 will look like a p.

Lastly, 0 is spelled zero. The 'z' in the word will remind you of the sound of z. This in turn has the same phonetic sounds as 's' and 'ce'. To remember this, think of the phrase 'zebra sees cello player.'

A QUICK TEST

Have you committed the sound to memory yet? Great! Now try a simple test for yourself. Next to each of the ten numbers given, write down in the blank spaces provided, their phonetic sounds. Please read the next section only after you have committed the phonetic sounds to memory.

Number	Phonetic Sound/Sounds	Number	Phonetic Sound/Sounds
1.	____________	6.	____________
2.	____________	7.	____________
3.	____________	8.	____________
4.	____________	9.	____________
5.	____________	10.	____________

USING PHONETIC SOUNDS

Now what do we do with all these phonetic sounds that we have just learnt? We will use them to create visual words from each set of numbers we are given. We do this by inserting vowels like 'a', 'e', 'i', 'o', 'u' as well as 'w', 'h' and 'y' (notice that it spells 'why') into the phonetic sounds of the numbers.

Let's look at a simple example. The number 21 is made up of the numbers 2 and 1. We learn that 2 has the sound 'n' (pronounced 'ne') and 1 has the sound of 't' (pronounced 'te'). Note that we could also use 'th' and 'd'. So 21 yields the sounds 'n', and 't' (sounds like 'ne' and 'te'). Notice that we can create a visual word 'net' if we add a vowel e in between the two phonetic sounds. Therefore, the number 21 is represented by the image of a net!

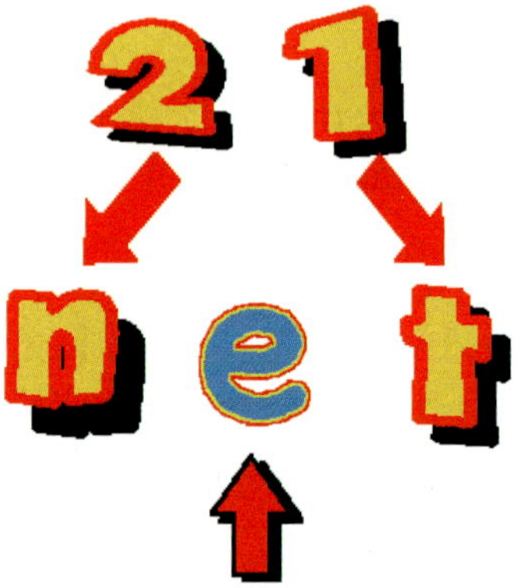

Let's try another example. The number 94 is made up of 9 and 4. 9 has the sound 'b' and 4 is represented by the sound 'r'. Thus, 94 has the sounds 'b' and 'r'. Can you think of any word you can form by inserting vowels into the phonetic sounds for 'b' and 'r'? Of course we can get the image bear by inserting the vowels e and a. Therefore the number 94 is represented by the visual image of a bear.

Notice that what we have been doing all along is to convert abstract numbers into images we can see in our mind!

WE ARE ONLY INTERESTED IN PHONETIC SOUNDS

Translates into

Ball → **95**

Take a look at the word 'ball'. If I were to ask you to do the reverse and convert that word to numbers based on the phonetic system, what would it be represented by? Many would say 955. Because the word 'ball' has one b (represented by 9) and two ls (l is represented by 5). Note that the letter a in 'ball' is not represented by any number since it is a vowel.

This is however a mistake! 'Ball' is represented, instead, by 95 (not 955) because in pronouncing 'ball', we use the sounds 'b' and 'l' only once each! Having two letter 'l's in 'ball' is irrelevant to generating the corresponding numbers because the second 'l' is silent.

Here's another example. What about the word 'knife'? Again, many people think that 'knife' contains the phonetic sounds 'k', 'n', 'f' ('i' and 'e' are vowels so they are not taken into consideration). Thus, it is represented by the number 728. This, too, is a mistake. 'K' is not included here because it is silent (you don't say the 'k' in 'knife'). Hence 'knife' is represented only by 28.

Knife

↓ **Translates into**

28

TEST YOURSELF!

Now that you understand the concept, work on the following.

EXERCISE 1

Use the Number System to convert each number to convert into a visual word.

Number	**Visual Image**
53	____________
21	____________
30	____________
541	____________
471	____________

EXERCISE 2

Convert the following words into the numbers represented by them.

Visual Image	**Number**
Dad	____________
Love	____________
Daze	____________
Mafia	____________
Check	____________

POSSIBLE ANSWERS TO THE EXERCISES

Have you done the exercise? Great! Here are some of my answers to the exercises. They may be different from yours, but it does not matter. You should learn to create your own unique word for each number and you will be alright as long as you follow the rules of the system. The numbers with phonetic sounds are underlined for you.

Number	Visual Image
1. 53	lime
2. 21	net, nod
3. 30	maize, mace
4. 541	lard
5. 471	rocket, racket (the 'k' is silent)

Visual Image	Number
1. dad	11
2. love	58
3. daze	10
4. mafia	38
5. check	67 (the 'k' is silent)

100 READY-TO-USE NUMBER PEGS

Now that you have learnt the phonetic sound of numbers, you can easily translate any number into key visual images (called pegs) which can be pictured and easily remembered.

To facilitate the use of the number system, create your own standard key visual images (pegs) for the first one hundred numbers. This way, every time you encounter a number between zero and one hundred, you will immediately know what visual image you can use to represent it. I have included below, the standard visual images I use for the first one hundred numbers. You can follow them, modify them or create your own!

1. Tie	21. Net	41. Rat	61. Jet	81. Fat
2. Noah	22. Nun	42. Rain	62. Chin	82. Fan
3. Ma	23. Name	43. Ram	63. Jam	83. Foam
4. Ray	24. Nero	44. Rear	64. Chair	84. Fur
5. Law	25. Nail	45. Rail	65. Jail	85. File
6. Jaw	26. Notch	46. Rash	66. Cha-Cha	86. Fish
7. Key	27. Neck	47. Rock	67. Jack	87. Fog
8. Ivy	28. Navy	48. Rafia	68. Chef	88. Fife
9. Bee	29. Knob	49. Rope	69. Chip	89. Fab
10. Toes	30. Mice	50. Lace	70. Case	90. Base
11. Dad	31. Mat	51. Lad	71. Cat	91. Bat
12. Tin	32. Man	52. Lion	72. Can	92. Bin
13. Dam	33. Mummy	53. Lime	73. Comb	93. Bomb
14. Deer	34. Mower	54. Lair	74. Car	94. Bar
15. Tail	35. Mail	55. Lily	75. Coal	95. Ball
16. Dish	36. Match	56. Leech	76. Cage	96. Beach
17. Deck	37. Mic(rophone)	57. Lake	77. Coco	97. Bike
18. Dive	38. Mafia	58. Lava	78. Cafe	98. Puff
19. Tap	39. Map	59. Lip	79. Cap	99. Baby
20. Nose	40. Rice	60. Jazz	80. Face	100. Daisies

Note that the letters in black are either vowels, letters that are silent (their sounds are not pronounced in their respective words) or letters that have not been defined as phonetic sounds of any numbers (i.e. such as 'w', 'h' and 'y').

APPLICATIONS OF THE NUMBER SYSTEM

As mentioned earlier, the Number System is a powerful tool which can be used to learn any subject that has anything relating to numbers. In this section, you will learn how to remember dates from history, memorize atomic numbers of elements and numerical values of any kind.

REMEMBERING DATES

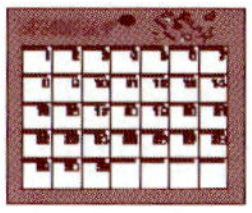

Studying History often requires students to remember when a particular event occured. There is thus a need to associate the event with the date (which is a series of numbers) when it occured.

How It Works

In order to remember dates or events, you must

1. form a visual image of the event that you want to remember
2. use the Number System to translate the date, which consists of numbers, to an appropriate key visual image
3. use an absurd story to link the visual image of the event to the key visual image of the date

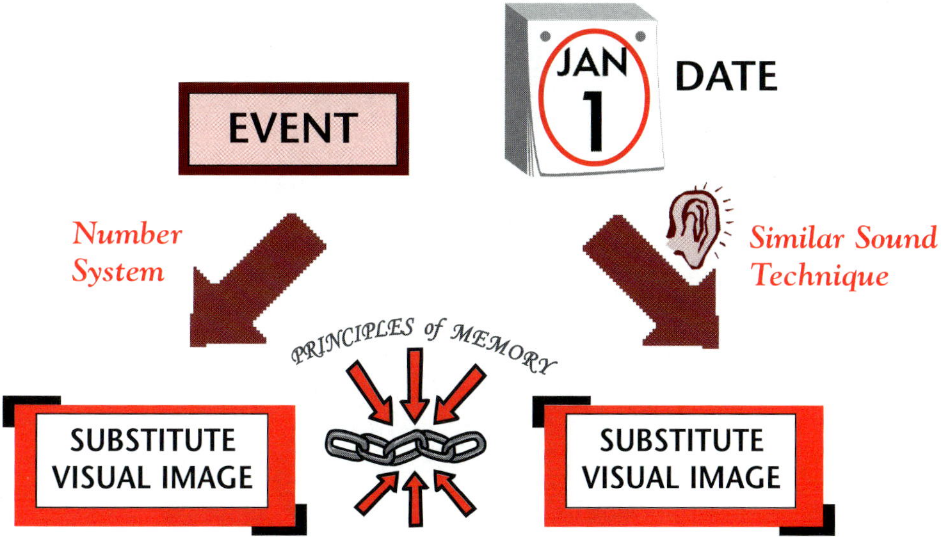

Example 1: Atomic Bomb

Say you need to remember that the first atomic bomb was dropped on 6 August 1945. As the event is the dropping of the first atomic bomb, the first step you need to take is to create a visual image of an atomic bomb in your mind.

Next, convert the date into its numerical equivalent, which is 6-8-45. Notice that we ignore the century (1900's), because you should be able to deduce the century through sheer logic. This leaves you to convert 6845 into visual images, based on the Number System you learnt earlier. One way is to pair the numbers into 68 and 45. As you know, 68 can be translated into 'chef' and 45 into 'rail'.

The last step is to make an absurd link between 'atomic bomb', 'chef' and 'rail'. So let's imagine that the first atomic bomb was built by a famous French chef who used old train rails as the main ingredient.

So every time you think of the first atomic bomb, you will be reminded of 'chef' and 'rail' which you can immediately translate to 6-8-45, which is 6 August 1945.

Example 2: Pearl Harbour

Suppose you wanted to remember that Pearl Harbour was bombed by the Japanese on 7 December 1941. Again, you can create a visual image of the event, which is the bombing of Pearl Harbour, by simply visualizing a string of pearls exploding.

Next, convert the date 7 December 1941 into 7-12-41 and use the Number System to translate the numbers 71241 into visual images. One way is to separate the numbers into three groups of 71, 24 and 1 and translate them into three visual images. This way, you will need to link up four images, the event image and three images for the date.

A faster way is to separate the numbers into 712 and 41. 712 can be translated into 'kitten' (one 't' is silent) and 41 can be translated into 'rat'. Finally link the images 'pearls exploding', 'kitten' and 'rat' together. Imagine that a string of pearls exploded and one of the beads hit a kitten which subsequently choked on a rat it was eating.

Now, every time you think of the bombing of Pearl Harbour, you will remember 71241 which translates in to 7 December 1941.

Dates In History To Practice On

This technique of remembering dates is not only a lot of fun, but also has lasting results. The explanation seems laborious but once you start, you will find that the actual process takes only a few seconds to execute in your mind.

Let's commit to memory dates listed below using the technique you have just learnt. Have a go!

	Event	Date
1.	Adolf Hitler's birth	20 April 1889
2.	Collapse of the Soviet Union	8 December 1991
3.	Franklin Roosevelt's election	1936
4.	The Great Depression	1929–1933

When you come across names of people or countries, convert them into a visual image using the Similar Sound Technique or the Trigger Technique. For example, 'Adolf' sounds like 'a dwarf'. So, Adolf Hitler can be represented by the visual image of a fierce dwarf with pointed ears. Similarly, 'Roosevelt' sounds like 'rooster belt'. So think of a rooster wearing a belt if you want to remember Franklin Roosevelt.

How about the Soviet Union? How do you visualize this country? One way is to use the Trigger Technique to represent the country using the images of a hammer and a sickle (a symbol found on the flag).

Test Yourself

In the space below, write down the dates of the events which you have just remembered and be sure to check if you have got them correct.

	Event	Date
1.	Adolf Hitler 's birth	____________
2.	Collapse of the Soviet Union	____________
3.	Franklin Roosevelt's election	____________
4.	The Great Depression	____________

REMEMBERING ATOMIC NUMBERS IN CHEMISTRY

Now let's see how we can remember the atomic numbers of elements in chemistry. Lets say you had to remember the following elements and their atomic numbers:

Element	Atomic Number
sodium	11
rubidium	37
tungsten	74
phosphorous	15

How It Works

What you need to do is to create a visual image for each element, using the Similar Sound Technique and a visual image for the corresponding atomic number using the Number System. You can then use the Link System to associate the image of the element with the image of the corresponding atomic number.

STEP 1: VISUALIZE THE ELEMENTS

Since the elements are abstract (we cannot see 'sodium'), we must use the Similar Sound Technique to come up with a visual word that sounds like the element to be remembered.

For example, 'sodium' sounds like 'sew dium'. (we can ignore 'dium' since most of the elements ends with a 'dium'). So, as a visual image, you can imagine yourself sewing with a needle and thread. This will remind you of the word 'sodium'.

Similarly, 'rubidium' sounds like 'ruby'. So you could imagine a big red sparkling ruby. How about 'tungsten'? It sounds like 'tongue stern'. You could imagine a tongue with a stern face. As for 'phosphorous', it sounds like 'forest'. So you could imagine a green forest.

Element	Visual Image
sodium	sew
rubidium	ruby
tungsten	stern tongue
phosphorous	forest

STEP 2: VISUALIZE THE ATOMIC NUMBERS

Next, convert the corresponding atomic numbers to visual images (words) using the Number System. In doing this, we get the following:

Atomic Number	Visual Image
11	Dad
37	mic
74	car
15	tail

STEP 2: LINK THE VISUAL IMAGES

Finally we link the visual image of the element with the visual image of the corresponding atomic number like this:

Image of element	Link	Image of Number
sew	⟷	Dad
ruby		mic
stern tongue		car
forest		tail

To link 'sew' and 'Dad', you could imagine yourself taking a needle and sewing your Dad's feet to the ground so he can't go to work. So every time you think of 'sodium' (sew), you will think of the atomic number 11 (represented by 'Dad').

To link 'ruby' and 'mic', imagine a million-dollar microphone made up of sparkling red rubies. So every time you think of 'rubidium', you will remember the atomic number 37.

Now, come up with your own absurd story to link the next two elements to their atomic numbers. When you are done, test your memory by filling in the table below. Have a go!

TEST YOUR MEMORY

Element	Atomic Number
sodium	____________
rubidium	____________
tungsten	____________
phosphorous	____________

REMEMBERING NUMERICAL VALUES

The Number System can be used to remember numerical values of any kind.

How It Works The method is similar to the way we remember dates in history and atomic numbers in chemistry. Simply link the visual image(s) of the key words to the visual image(s) of the numbers involved.

EXAMPLE 1: HOW FAR IS THE MOON?

Suppose you have to remember that the Moon is 384 630 km from the earth, the first step is to create a visual image of the moon, since 'moon' is the key word.

The second step is to translate the number 384 630 into visual images. One way is to separate them into 38, 46 and 30. These three numbers translate into the images 'mafia', 'rash' and 'mice', respectively.

Finally, use a ridiculous story to link up the images for 'moon', 'mafia', 'rash' and 'mice'. Imagine that in order for you to go to the moon, you have to engage the services of a mafia chief with a rash, caused by mice that can fly you to the moon.

Remembering this story will remind you that the distance of the moon from the earth is 384 630 kilometres.

EXAMPLE 2: WHAT IS THE SPEED OF LIGHT?

To remember that the speed of light is 3 x 10^8 metres per second, form a visual image of light travelling very fast.

Next, translate 3108 into visual images. One way is to separate it into the numbers 310 and 8, which translate into 'mats' and 'ivy' respectively.

Finally link the images of 'light', 'mats' and 'ivy' togther. To do this, imagine a beam of light travelling very fast on long mats made of ivy.

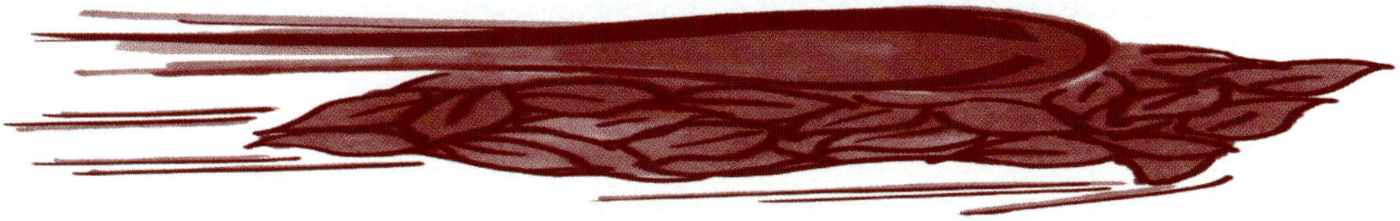

Numerical Values To Practice On

You are now ready for some practice. Look at the list below and use the Number System to remember the numerical values given.

1. The boiling point of liquid is 78 degrees Celsius.
2. The value of π is approximately 3.142.
3. The density of oxygen is 1.43 kilogramme metre cube.
4. The average rainfall in Singapore is 2 413 millilitres a year.
5. The area of the African continent is 30 320 000 square kilometres.

TIPS

Notice that it would be impractical to form a visual image of the last four zeros found in 30 320 000 sq km (the last practice example) using the Number System. In such instances, where a number (normally zeros) is repeated many times, you have to be flexible and creative in forming your own visual images. You could, for example, represent the last four zeros as four eggs (zeros look like eggs).

TEST YOUR MEMORY

Are you ready to test your ability to remember numerical values? Good, here is your chance. In the spaces provided, write down the appropriate numerical values and be sure to check your answers when you are done.

1. The boiling point of liquid is ______ degrees Celsius.
2. The value of π is approximately ____________ .
3. The density of oxygen is ________ kilogram metre cube.
4. The average rainfall in Singapore is _________ millilitres.
5. The area of the African continent is ___________ square kilometres.

A FINAL WORD MEMORY SYSTEMS

The usefulness of the Link System and the Number System is by no means limited to the examples you have seen here. They can be used to remember any subject matter. It is up to you to be creative and experiment with the different ways of modifying and applying the memory systems. Remember, as long as you follow the principles of visualization and association through absurdity, you will develop supermemory! Now, discover more about your memory in the chapter on memory patterns.

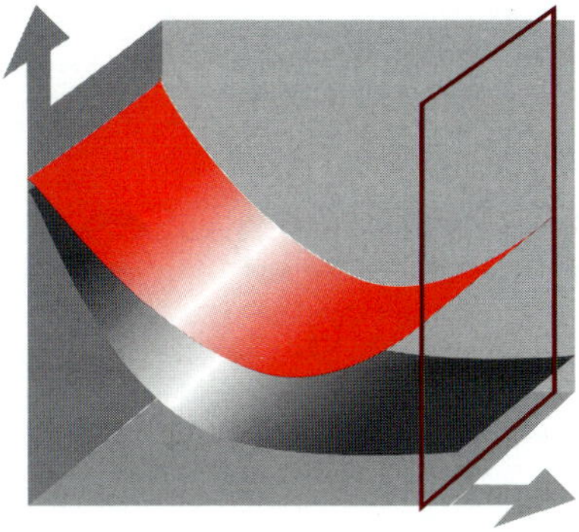

CHAPTER 8

THE PATTERN OF MEMORY

Do you know that your memory follows a certain cyclical pattern? Knowing this, you will understand why there are times when you are able to learn easily and effectively, while there are other times when you feel as though your memory is saturated and no matter how long you stare at your book, nothing seems to be going in. By understanding your memory pattern, you will be able to make efficient use of your study time.

DISCOVERING YOUR MEMORY PATTERN

Let me take you through a short experiment that will allow you to discover your own memory pattern. Read through the list of words given below only once and without using any memory principles and systems, do your best to remember as many of them as possible.

right	may	to
from	is	far
five	why	for
him	the	is
cute	if	left
the	is	the
soar	been	maize
is	the	ring
the	Santa Claus	baby
row	can	goal
the	the	ruler

Now, without looking back at the list, write down as many items as you can remember in the blank spaces provided. You do not have to recall them in sequence.

1. ________	9. ________	17. ________	25. ________	33. ________
2. ________	10. ________	18. ________	26. ________	
3. ________	11. ________	19. ________	27. ________	
4. ________	12. ________	20. ________	28. ________	
5. ________	13. ________	21. ________	29. ________	
6. ________	14. ________	22. ________	30. ________	
7. ________	15. ________	23. ________	31. ________	
8. ________	16. ________	24. ________	32. ________	

Look at the list you have just made. If you did not use any memory systems, you would probably have left out a number of words. But look at the words you remembered. Why did you tend to remember those words and not the others? If you look closely, you will find a pattern to the way you remember. In general, in any period of learning, you will tend to:

1. Remember things at the beginning of a learning period.
   So you probably would have remembered the first three to five words.

2. Remember things that appear toward the end of a learning period.
   You probably wrote down the last three to five words.

3. Remember things that are repeated.
   Such as 'is' and 'the'.

4. Remember things that stand out.
   You would probably have easily recalled 'Santa Claus'.

5. Remember things that are associated or related.
   You would probably have recalled 'left' and 'right'.

Therefore, if we were to plot a graph of 'percentage recalled' against 'time', it would yield the following graphs.

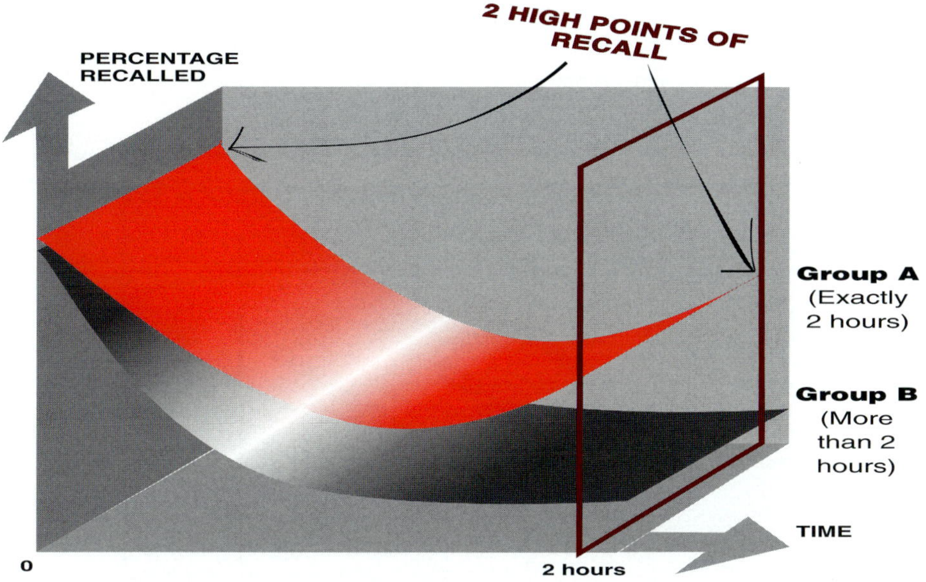

We can see from the above graph that in any period of study of up to two hours (see graph A), there are be only two high points of recall: at the beginning and at the end. During the middle of a study period, there is a dip in the percentage of content recalled. So, in any period of study, a lot of what you are learning in the middle would probably be forgotten The longer the study period, the larger the dip.

If you were to study for more than two hours continuously (see graph B), there would only be one significant high point of recall, and you would be wasting your time. This is why many students experience reaching a point where they feel that their mind is saturated and incapable of absorbing anything else.

AN OPTIMAL STUDY SESSION

Research, has shown that the ideal length of an entire study session should be no more than two hours. This session should be broken up into four, twenty-five minute or thirty-minute periods. In between each period, you should take a break of about between two and five minutes.

During these short breaks, you should do some relaxation exercises. After each study session of two hours, you should relax for at least thirty minutes before starting again.

In this way (as shown in the diagram below), you will have eight high points of recall and the dip in percentage of recall for each learning period would be much less. The result would be a greater ability to recall, and a more efficient use of your study time.

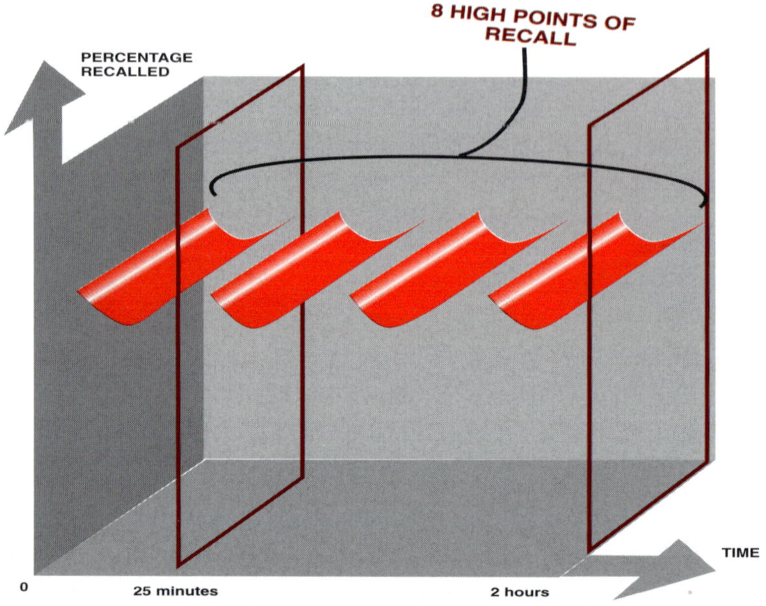

'CRAMMING' DOES NOT WORK

Many students I have come to know believe that it is useless to start studying early, because they would simply forget everything well before the examinations and would therefore have to study everything all over again. These students believe that they should only study about five days before each paper and, if they are lucky, they would have time for one revision, before the examination.

As such, they often do badly or go blank during the exam, getting their facts confused and making very careless (and unnecessary) mistakes.

To me this is a suicidal way of studying because it goes against all the principles of effective learning. Studying at the last minute will probably involve long hours, without the luxury of being able to take breaks, and will result in low recall ability.

In addition, the students' knowledge of facts would probably be very muddled and their memory links, weak because they are constantly adding new information before their minds have had the chance to organize and integrate what they have already learnt. This new information could well interfere with existing information, causing greater havoc!

Furthermore, as a result of last-minute studying, they are not relaxed, and are therefore unable to learn well.

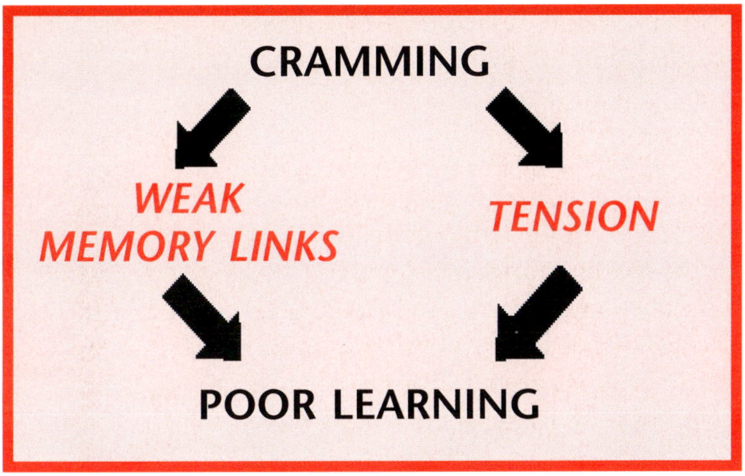

So, if you were to start preparation early and spread out your study time, how do you keep your memory at its peak until the examination day? The answer is through revision.

Many students think that revision is a waste of time, but done strategically, with Mind Maps®, it should save you more time than your normal method of study. Not only that, the more revision you do, the greater your understanding, the stronger your memory links and the greater your skill in the subject.

Very often, we may know a concept, or how to solve a problem, but during the examination, we become confused and make all sorts of mistakes. The reason for this is insufficient mastery of the skills to a level of unconscious competence. The only way to achieve this level of mastery is through thorough revision.

You can be well versed in the art of *kung fu*, theoretically, but if you have not mastered it through actual practice, you will probably end up losing a fight. Many students, however, go into battle only armed with the knowlege but not the skills to tackle questions or apply knowledge.

YOU FORGET 80% WITHIN 24 HOURS

Studies have shown that if revision is not done within twenty-four hours of initial study, eighty percent of what has been learned will be forgotten.

This is the reason why many students who study early but do not revise within twenty-four hours, complain that they have forgotten almost everything before the examination. Any attempt to revise just before the examination is like starting all over again. Revision would take almost as much time as it did in the original period of study because most of what was supposedly learned would have been forgotten.

This does not mean that we should not start learning early. What it means is that we should revise at the right time, while our memory is still at its peak. In this way, revision would take a very short time and it would further strengthen the memory links put in place earlier. In fact, revision should take five to ten minutes for every hour of initial study time.

STRATEGIC REVISION

Revision should take place at specific times after a learning period. The first revision should begin ten minutes after initial learning. This is because research has shown that recall tends to peak ten minutes after learning, before declining steadily. The next revision should be within twenty-four hours, a week, a month and after the sixth month, respectively, if necessary. This schedule will keep the memory at its peak. The graph below provides a summary of the optimum revision schedule.

Ideally, you should start preparing for an examination about a month before it. This means you will go through about four revision periods. You should time your revision such that the last revision period falls on the day before the examination. However, much depends on your revision schedule and the number of subjects you are studying.

The Optimum Revision Schedule

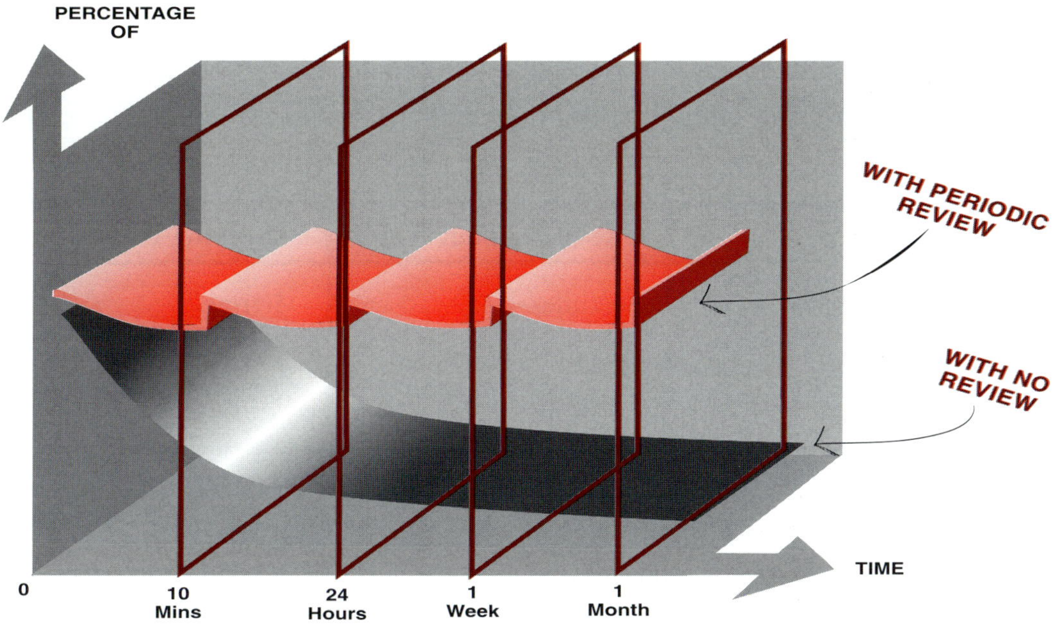

REVISION SAVES YOU TIME

You are probably thinking to yourself, 'If I follow this method of revising four times before the examintion, wouldn't it take up a lot more time than the normal method of revising just once before?' The answer is 'No'.

Remember, if you were to follow the conventional way of studying once and then once more before the examination, more than eighty percent of the facts would have been forgotten. This means that your revision time would be just as long as your initial study time. Not only that, but because you did not revise while everything was still fresh in your mind, the revision would be quite useless in reinforcing what was studied.

So, if you originally took two hours to study a chapter, you would probably take at least one-and-a-half hours to go over it. Thus, you would take a total of three-and-a-half hours to complete a chapter.

If you were to revise four times, your initial study period would still take two hours, but your first revision (within ten minutes) would take you only ten minutes. This is because the facts should be still very fresh in your mind.Your second revision (within twenty-four hours) should take you another fifteen minutes.

The third revision which should be done one week later, should again take you less than fifteen minutes. The final revision, on the day before the examination, should take you less than ten minutes.

If you add up all four revision time periods, you would take a total of two hours and fifty minutes which is forty minutes less than the conventional method. But, more importantly, because each revision was done at the time when all the facts were still fresh in your mind, your comprehension of the material is four times better than revision done according to the conventional method.

	Revising Four Times	Revising once
Number of Revisions	4 times	1 time
Total Time	2 hours 50 minutes	$3\frac{1}{2}$ hours
Comprehension	4 times better	

Congratulations! You have just learned two of the most powerful learning techniques around, the Mind Map® and the Memory Systems. Master them and you can expect to yield the results you desire. Now that you are equipped with the tools to battle the examination, let's move on to goal setting.

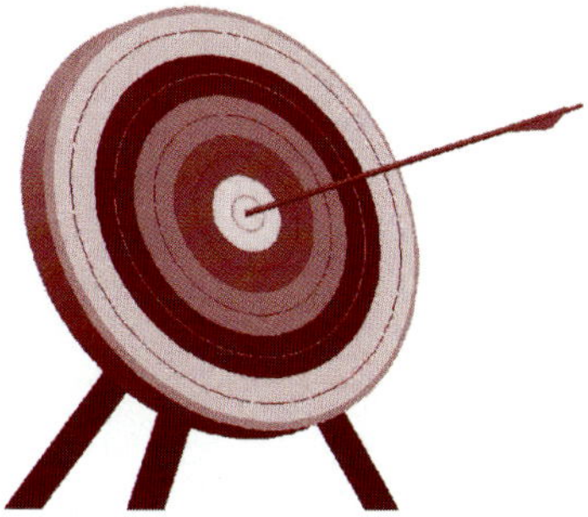

CHAPTER 9

THE SECRET OF GOALS

In my days as an underachiever, I sometimes wondered how and where my successful classmates found the drive and motivation to finish their homework, or to study thoroughly for a test. How could they study for long hours, even on weekends, giving up shopping, films and fun? They did this and easily reaped good results while the rest of us were led astray by T.V, video games, going to parties and other temptations. We could never imagine sacrificing our precious freedom on study.

What was the secret of these high achievers? Where did they find the motivation to work so hard? Let me share this secret with you. All successful students have compelling goals that give them the power to overcome laziness and distractions. Yes, goals have the power to drive us to work throughout the day and night. They empower us.

There is no such thing as a lazy student, only one who does not have a clear goal!

GOALS ENERGIZE US

You're probably wondering, 'Do goals really energize us?' Well, think about this. Have you ever felt very excited planning for a big date, a birthday celebration or an exciting trip abroad? How did you feel the night before? Did you feel so excited and energized that you could not get to sleep?

All that energy you had came from that powerful goal you were working towards. Now, imagine if you could direct that same kind of energy towards studying. How much more could you achieve then?

GOALS DIRECT OUR LIVES

The goals you have drive you and direct how you live your life at every moment. They direct the decisions you make and the actions you will take. Whatever you're doing, be it studying, watching a film or just lazing about what you achieve all depends on the goals you have.

Analysing my goals during my days as a 'lazy student', I found that they were to avoid the 'frustration' of studying, watching the latest films, sleeping whenever I could and avoiding failing the examinations.

No wonder I had deplorable results! My goals were directing me away from studying. They were directing me to laze about and watch films and T.V. The goal of avoiding failure in the examinations hardly gave me the inspiration and energy to obtain good results. If you don't consciously design goals that will inspire you and direct your life to success, you will subconsciously develop these self-sabotaging goals.

You must consciously design goals that will drive and direct you to success.

IF YOU *CAN'T* SEE IT YOU *CAN'T* HIT IT!

If I were to come up to you one day and challenge you to a game of darts, would you take me on? Probably, if you were much better at it than I am. What if I told you that you had to be blindfolded so as to give me a better chance of winning? No way, you say. You'd think it would be terribly unfair. How could you be expected to hit the target if you are not even given the chance to see it, you ask.

How does this relate to your life? Well, have you ever wondered how you can possibly reach the target of obtaining distinctions if you do not first see the target or goal in your mind?

LESSONS ON LIFE

The Power Of Goal Setting

In 1953, a survey was carried out on the graduating class of Yale University (USA). Its purpose was to find out how many of the graduating students had set financial goals for the future. The survey revealed that only three percent of the students had set goals. Twenty years later, a follow-up survey was conducted. It traced all those past students who were then in their forties. Guess what? It was found that the combined income of the three percent who had set goals was greater than the total combined income of the ninety-seven percent who had not set any goals!

EMPOWERING GOALS

Goals must be set in a certain way before they can have the power to motivate us to see them through. Many new year resolutions are seldom followed through simply because they were not set in an empowering way. They were nothing more than a weak wish or desire, hardly compelling at all. For our goals to be empowering, they must be have the following characteristics:

1 BIG & EXCITING

Set big goals, not small ones like, 'I want to pass that test'. It is too puny to excite you. Big goals may seem to be out of reach at the time, but the thought of accomplishing them will excite and drive you. People who set small goals for themselves do so for fear of not reaching them, and often lead limited and boring lives.

All of us have different passions in life. Find out what excites and drives you and make that a reason for you to achieve your goal.

2 REALISTIC

Goals must be realistic, too. Setting a goal to get 'A's is not being unrealistic even if you are currently getting 'C's and 'D's. Sure, it will take you a lot of time and effort to attain 'A's, but that is within your control. What is unrealistic, for example, is finding ways and means of making the marker more lenient.

3 STATED IN THE PRESENT CONTINUOUS TENSE

When you write down your goals in a way that suggests that they are being realized, it puts you in the best mental frame to bring those goals into reality. Therefore, if you want to set a goal to get an 'A' for history, you should write it down as "I am scoring an 'A' for history, and am feeling really good about myself". If you state your goal in future tense (e.g. I will score an 'A' for history) your subconscious mind will intepret it as a future outcome, and it has been found to work in such a way that the future will always remain the future. So remember, state your goals as if they are occurring now!

4 STATED POSITIVELY

For your goals to be effective, they must be stated positively. For example, don't set a goal to 'not fail physics' rather set a goal to 'pass physics'. You see, your mind cannot process negative commands (like the word 'not') and will guide you to whatever you focus on. If you focus on 'not failing', you will keep on failing!

5 WRITTEN DOWN

You must be reminded of your goals daily. So, write them down where you will see them every day. The best thing to do is to make a poster of your goals and stick it up in your room.

LESSONS ON LIFE

If You Can See It, You Can Read It.

An old friend of mine whom I had met in the Super-Teen® programme went one step further than stating his goals in the present continuous tense. Bruce gave himself straight 'A's in his report card, even before he sat for the examination.

What Bruce did was to dig up an old report card and with the help of correction fluid, replaced all his previous grades with the 'A' grades he wanted for the coming exams. Next, he changed the date on the report card to reflect that of the coming examination. Finally, he pasted his remodelled report card on his bathroom mirror so he could see it every day. Seeing his 'A' results created an optimum mental state in him and he went on to score six 'A's and a 'B'! He was only off the mark for one subject.

7 STEPS TO GOAL SETTING

Goals should be set for all aspects of your life to make you an all-round person. You should set academic goals, career goals, financial goals, family goals and relationship goals.

Now let me take you through the steps in goal-setting. There are altogether seven of these:

1 WRITE SPECIFICALLY WHAT YOU WANT

Goals must be very specific. Don't write down 'I want to do better in Geography'. If you are not specific, your mind will wonder, 'How much better than before? Five marks better or ten? Do I want an 'A' or a 'B'?' So, you must give your mind a specific command.

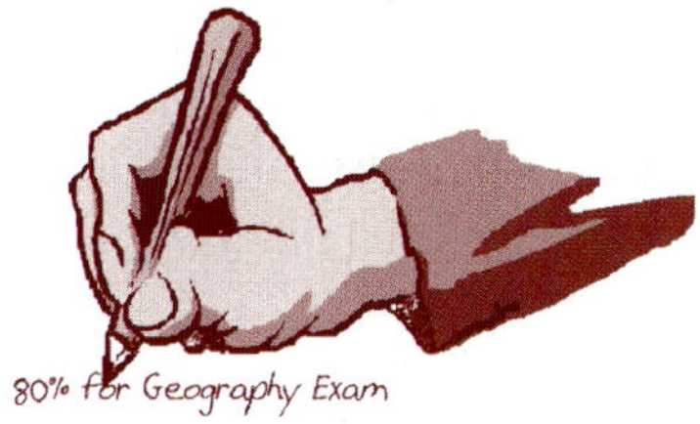

Example: 'I am committed to achieving 76% in maths.'

2 LIST ALL THE BENEFITS & REASONS FOR ACHIEVING THAT GOAL

Write down all the benefits you will get from achieving your goal, making sure it is exciting to you! It is important that the reasons or benefits you give are passionate.

Example: 'to gain recognition and respect' or 'to get into the college of my choice.'

3 LIST WHAT YOU WOULD LOSE IF YOU DON'T FOLLOW THROUGH

This should create enough pain to drive you to take action.

Example: 'I won't be able to get into a good junior college and do the course I want or my four years in school would be wasted.'

4 WRITE ABOUT YOUR PRESENT SITUATION

In this step you must write down where you are now, as compared to where you want to be. This will give you an idea of how much more effort you will have to put in, and how effective your current strategies are.

Example: 'I am now scoring an average of 60% for Chemistry and I need to improve my grade by 20% to hit my goal of 80% for the final exams.'

5 WRITE ABOUT YOUR STRATEGY & PLAN OF ACTION

Write down the strategies you intend to use and a detailed plan of how you are going to carry out those strategies. A personal organizer with a calendar is ideal for such planning.

Example:

a) My strategy is to make Mind Maps® for my history textbook and use memory techniques to remember the information.

b) My plan of action is to make two Mind Map® a day for the next two weeks. I will then spend three hours a day memorizing the information for another week.

6 WRITE DOWN YOUR MILESTONE GOALS

Milestone goals are the smaller goals that lead up to your main goal. Identify what these milestone goals are. How well you achieve these milestone goals will enable you to assess and realign your study strategies.

Example: 'My milestone goals are that I am scoring 80% in my four continual assessment papers and my preliminary examinations.'

You must be very specific. Don't write down 'I want to do better in Geography'. If you are not specific, your mind will wonder, 'How much better than before? Five marks better or ten? Do I want an 'A' or a 'B'?' So, you must give your mind a specific command.

Example: 'I am committed to achieving 76% in maths.'

7 SET A DEADLINE

You must set a specific date for achieving your goal because without a deadline, you will lose focus and procrastinate till the goal is forgotten. Setting a specific date means writing down not only the year and the month, but the very day you plan to reach your target.

Example: 'I will accomplish this goal on 15 April 1999.'

AN EXAMPLE OF EFFECTIVE GOAL SETTING

Let's look at a sample of a goal set on the final examination for Mathematics.

Step 1:
I am committed to achieving 79% in mathematics for my '0' level examinations.

Step 2:
This is so that I will be able to get into the science course in junior college. I will prove to my teachers that I can score a distinction in maths.

Step 3:
I may not accumulate enough marks to enter the junior college or the course of my choice. I may even end up in a job that is below my expectations.

Step 4:
I am now scoring on average of 60% for my maths tests. I need to improve my grade by 19%.

Step 5:
My strategy is to work on examination papers from the past six years so that I can score 90% for each one. I will practise at least once a week and I aim to score 80% in my mid-year examination. I will spend two hours a day revising maths.

Step 6:
My milestone goal is to score 90% in my four continual assessments and my preliminary examinations.

Step 7:
The date for accomplishing my goals is 26 November 1999.

A GOAL POSTER

It is also very useful to draw up a goal poster. Simply list all your examination goals on a single sheet of paper and put it up where you will see it every day. You will be constantly reminded of and focused on your mission.

For the goal poster, simply define each goal specifically, list the benefits and reasons for its accomplishment and write down your deadline. In other words, you only need to include steps 1, 2 and 7. An example is shown below.

Step 1:
'O' Level Examination 1999 Results

English	*70%*
Mathematics	*79%*
Physics	*80%*
Chemistry	*77%*
Second Language	*65%*
Geography	*76%*
History	*76%*

Step 2:
My reasons are to get into Victoria Junior College and get into the science course. I want to prove to my friends and teachers that I can attain top results.

Step 3:
The date for accomplishing my goals is 26 Nov 98.

YOUR MOVE!

Are you ready to begin designing the kind of results you want and the life you will ultimately lead? Good. Remember that you have all the potential and resources to produce exceptional results. So design your life with passion and absolute faith! To get you started, I want you to set a goal for your most challenging subject. Go through all seven steps of goal setting, writing down your goals in the spaces provided and have fun doing it!

1. Define your goal specifically.

2. List down the benefits & reasons for achieving it.

3. Write what you stand to lose.

4. Write down your present situation.

5. Write down your strategy & plan of action.

6. What are your milestone goals?

7. Write down the date of accomplishment.

Have you finished setting your goal? Great! Now, I want you to design a goal poster for your upcoming examination. Follow the guidelines given below, then redraw it on a big piece of poster paper with a lot of colours and images. Stick it up in your room when it is complete.

Step 1:
Write down the name of your upcoming examination below.

____

Next, list the subjects you are taking and your expected grades.

	SUBJECT	GRADE
1.	____________________	__________
2.	____________________	__________
3.	____________________	__________
4.	____________________	__________
5.	____________________	__________
6.	____________________	__________
7.	____________________	__________

Step 2:
Write down the reasons for & benefits of scoring those grades.

1. ________________________________
2. ________________________________
3. ________________________________
4. ________________________________
5. ________________________________

Step 3:
Write down when you will accomplish the results.

____

SET A GOAL, AND YOUR MIND WILL FIND A WAY!

In goal setting, one of the most important beliefs you must have is that whatever you can conceive and believe, you will be able to achieve. As you plan your life, do so with absolute faith and expectation.

Even if at this point in time you are unsure of how you are going to be able to achieve the goal, it does not matter! Set it anyway! If you can find enough reasons why you want to achieve it, your mind will eventually lead you towards deciding how to do it. Goals actually make our mind alert and receptive to opportunities all around us. Without goals, we tend to let such opportunities in life slip by.

So, if all these goals are in place, does this mean that we will definitely succeed? You cannot be absolutely certain of it. If our goals are not followed up by concrete action, they will forever remain dreams. But if you act on them, they will become your destiny. So how do we get youselves to act? Find out in the next chapter on how you can spur yourself on.

CHAPTER 10

MOTIVATION — MOVING BEYOND PROCRASTINATION

MOVING BEYOND PROCRASTINATION

How many times have you established a goal or made a resolution, but never got started on achieving it? Or how many times have you got started on something, only to lose interest and stamina by the end of the first day?

We all know what we should do in life, like studying for that big examination, but somehow, we never get round to doing it, until it is too late. This habit, procrastination, affects just about everybody. It is simply paralysis in taking action that we know will benefit us.

Procrastination is the main saboteur of all success. You can set the most inspiring goals and plan the perfect timetable but if you fail to act when you are supposed to, then you would have already failed.

When you procrastinate, don't you also get this feeling that your life is being controlled rather than you having control over it? Your sense of fear tells us to stop watching T.V. and to get started on that school project, but a compelling force drives us you watch one more programme. In order to overcome procrastination, you must learn how to control it, instead of letting it control you.

THE FORCES OF PAIN & PLEASURE

The forces that drive any behaviour are those of pain and pleasure. We always behave in a way that will move us away from what we think is painful and towards what we think will be pleasurable. Why do we keep putting off doing a project till the last minute even though we know we should start early? Well, because most of us have been conditioned to link massive pain with doing the project now (the pain of stress, frustration and giving up our favourite TV programmes) and link pleasure with doing something else, like watching TV.

How do we eventually get around to doing it? Normally we start taking action when the project is due the next day or when we suddenly face pressure from peers who have finished it. But why are we able to act now and not earlier? Again, it is because we now perceive that not doing our project now will bring us more pain (the pain of not being able to finish on time and producing a bad report) and this overrides the short term pain of doing the project now.

TAKE CHARGE OF YOUR LIFE

Instead of being a slave to pain and pleasure, take charge of your life and use the same forces to drive you to take the action that you want, like to start studying consistently, to watch your diet and to finish your project well before the due date! The quality of your behaviour depends on what you have consciously or subconsciously linked pain and pleasure to. Nothing is, by itself, pleasurable or painful but it is what we link it with that makes it so. Successful students have learned to link pleasure with studying and pain with not studying. These people never procrastinate and always score 'A's.

Others have, instead, been conditioned to link a lot of pain with studying and a lot of pleasure with avoiding studying. These people always procrastinate and are never able to follow through on their plans and goals. In trying to overcome their procrastination, they try all sorts of methods, but these methods don't address the root of the problem. In their minds, they still link pain with studying and pleasure with avoiding it. This is why, no matter how hard they try, they always end up procrastinating again.

So, the key to changing any behaviour, whether it is to stop smoking or to overcome procrastination is to change what you link pain and pleasure with. You have to learn to link pleasure with studying now and pain with putting it off. So right now, let's see how we do that.

REWIRE YOUR MIND

First, identify what present behaviour you would like to change and what new behaviour or action you want to replace it with. For example, you may want to change your present behaviour of putting off studying till the last minute (procrastinating) with a new behaviour of doing it immediately.

In the next exercise, you will learn how to link massive amounts of pain to procrastinating and great pleasure to taking immediate action.

Reconditioning your mind to act now

YOUR MOVE!

STEP **1**

Write down in the space below, all the pain you will possibly experience if you continue to put off studying for a test or examination. For example, you may eventually feel the pain of failing and being retained or being ridiculed by your teachers, relatives and friends. Write down as many of these painful outcomes as you can, making sure that they are enough to upset you.

All the pain that I will feel if I continue with my old behaviour (e.g. procrastinating)

1.
2.
3.
4.
5.
6.
7.

STEP 2

Use your imagination and actually see in your mind's eye, all the pain you would eventually experience as a result of procrastinating and studying only at the last minute using the ideas you jotted down earlier. In your imagined experience, I want you to actually see what you would see, hear what you would hear and feel what you would feel, going through all that pain.

This exercise is intended to create enough emotion to drive you to change your behaviour. For example, imagine yourself having scored low grades. See your friends with their high grades. Feel the regret, anger and frustration of not having studied earlier. Feel the agony of not being able to get into the school or course of your choice. Visualize yourself being reprimanded by parents and teachers and despised by classmates whom you admire. Create as many painful feelings as possible and make the pain seem as real as possible to you.

TAKE THREE MINUTES AND DO IT NOW.

Next, I want you to imagine what your life will be like five years from now as a result of your procrastination. I want you to imagine the worst possible scenario. You could see yourself as a dropout, with no friends and no job, regretting your past behaviour. Again, use sight, sound and feelings to create experiences that seems real.

TAKE THREE MINUTES AND DO IT NOW.

As you begin to feel compelled to overcome procrastination, you can now imagine what your life will be like ten years from now as a result of procrastination. Again, imagine the worst possible scenario and make it as real as possible. For example, you could see yourself in a lowly paid job and with few friends.

TAKE THREE MINUTES AND DO IT NOW.

Why are you doing this? Because you'd only start to regret and wish you could change things when it is too late. It's only when you have no education, no money and no prospects that you begin to say, 'If only I had...'. Unfortunately at this stage, it is too late. So, before this happens, create the painful consequences for yourself so you can take immediate action, instead of wishing you could.

STEP 3

The next step is to link as much pleasure as possible to the new behaviour that you want. First write down all the pleasurable feelings or experiences you will enjoy if you studied consistently. Do this in the space below.

All the pleasure that I will happen with my new behaviour (e.g. taking immediate action).

1.
2.
3.
4.
5.
6.
7.

STEP 4

Again, this is a very important step in the process of reconditioning yourself. Use your imagination and see yourself as if you were already feeling and experiencing all that wonderful pleasure that comes with studying early. Imagine yourself receiving a report card with all the results that you want. It's your passport to success and happiness.

Feel the satisfaction and joy of holding your well deserved results and seeing them before your very own eyes. See yourself being congratulated and praised by your parents, friends and teachers. Make the experience as real as possible for yourself!

TAKE THREE MINUTES AND DO IT NOW

When you think about studying now, it should evoke a more positive response than it did before. Now, I want you to imagine your life five years the date you began to start studying consistently. You can see yourself in a prestigious university enjoying all the benefits that you desire.

TAKE THREE MINUTES AND DO IT NOW

Lastly, see yourself ten years from now in a respectable job which your particularly enjoy. Make the experience, together with all these wonderful sensations, as real as possible.

TAKE THREE MINUTES AND DO IT NOW

STEP 5

In the final step, you need to break your old habit of doing things and condition yourself towards accepting your new behaviour. Starting right now, make it a point to do things that you normally would not do, or change your sequence of doing things. Instead of vegetating in front of the television or taking a nap straight after school, do a quick review of the day's work or read a book. You may even consider going for a quick jog or working out with weights.

We are all creatures of habit and need to break whatever behavioural pattern is limiting our success. Finally, repeat the two imagination exercises regularly (at least twice a week) until you have conditioned your new behaviour and made it a part of your new pattern of behaviour.

LESSONS ON LIFE

How Catherine overcame procrastination

One of my friends Catherine, shared with me her way of overcoming procrastination. Catherine was the top Commerce student of Temasek Junior College (a top-ranking junior college in Singapore) for two years. She valued both her sleep and her time for going out. She is aware that if she kept putting off doing her work, it would mean less sleep later on, and less time for going out. In actual fact, she was subconsciously linking massive pain with putting off her work and pleasure with starting it immediately. This simple process drove her to make optimal use of her time and it earned her a top position in the National University of Singapore.

MORE TIPS ON TAKING ACTION...NOW!

Besides the mind conditioning exercises, here are a few other things you can do to get moving beyond procrastination. All these tips are based on the same principle: linking pain with procrastination and linking pleasure with taking action.

1 MAKE A COMMITMENT TO YOURSELF.

The best way to compel yourself to take action is to make a personal commitment that you will take action to achieve your goals. Everybody wants straight 'A's, but not many are committed to working towards getting them. The difference between wanting something and being committed to it is that commitment involves doing whatever it takes to achieve it. It means that it takes precedence over anything else and is your priority. If you want to realize your goals, you must first be sure that you are committed to achieving them and not merely wanting it.

You must put your commitment in writing in the same way you set your goals. Sign this statement and get your best friend or your parents to endorse the statement as witnesses. Next, put up the contract you have just made on your mirror, so you can be reminded of it every day.

2 PUBLICIZE YOUR COMMITMENT.

Making a personal commitment is powerful, but it is not enough. This is because most people manage to find excuses to break promises they've made to themselves. So, make a public commitment.

Tell all your friends, teachers, parents and even your relatives that you will score seven 'A's in your examinations. Will they laugh at you?

But instead of feeling bad about it, use their mockery to drive yourself! In fact, the more they laugh, the better! By putting your reputation on the line, you have no choice but to act.

3 CONSTANTLY REVIEW YOUR GOALS.

Review your goals daily, especially your specific wants and your reasons, and the benefits of achieving them. This will keep your mind focused and give you direction. Very often, external forces may misdirect you so reviewing your goals puts you on track.

4 REWARD YOURSELF ALONG THE WAY.

It is important to give yourself small rewards as you achieve each milestone goal. Even when you achieve something as small as doing well in a class test or finishing an assignment on time, reward yourself. Take a break by going to the beach or by watching TV.

Similarly, punish yourself whenever you procrastinate. If you procrastinate and don't finish a tutorial by the deadline, make yourself stay up the next night to finish it. In fact, forgo your favourite television programme if you have to.

CHAPTER 11

FORMULAE FOR SCORING 'A's

Most average students I know believe that high-achievers use some secret formula for studying. After all, these top students seem to start studying for the examination at about the same time as the rest, but they seem to master the subjects much more easily, and are able to perform at their peak during the examination. In this section, I will share with you these study formulae. They are the result of my modelling the common steps that all successful students take to get an edge over the rest.

FORMULA 1: BE CONSISTENT

The first thing I found that was common to all 'A' students was that they were consistent in their schoolwork throughout the entire school year. This means that at any one point in time, they would be prepared to answer any question, on any topic that has been taught.

The way these students maintained their consistency was to ensure that they fully understood a topic that was taught, before the teacher moved on to the next topic. If they weren't sure about something, they would ask questions.

TIPS ON BEING CONSISTENT

Here are some useful steps you can take to ensure that you keep up during the school year. I have found that they are used instinctively by all successful students.

1 READ AHEAD OF YOUR TEACHER

Find out what your teacher will be teaching next and read that topic, making Mind Maps® and other notes before you actually attend the lesson.

2 BE ATTENTIVE & ASK QUESTIONS

During the lesson, you should clear any doubts or ask any questions you may have when you first read through that topic.

If the teacher covers information that you have missed out in your reading, then add that new data to your Mind Maps®.

3 ALWAYS COMPLETE YOUR HOMEWORK BEFORE CLASS

By doing your homework before it is discussed in class, you will make the best use of your time. You will find out where your weakness in the subject lies, and be able to address the problems early. In addition, homework will help you find out if you've understood concepts taught.

4 ALWAYS CLARIFY MISTAKES YOU MAKE IN YOUR HOMEWORK

If you make a mistake in your work, do not just leave at that. Find out where you went wrong. If you make a mistake now, you are very likely to repeat it in your examinations.

Contrary to what most students think, good students do not make fewer mistakes than poor students. In fact, they make more mistakes than anybody else. The only difference is that they make their mistakes during their self-practice sessions and learn from their mistakes before the examinations.

MISTAKES ARE THE BEST TEACHERS

When you make mistakes in your homework, assignments and class tests, it does not mean that you are condemned to a life time of failure and will never do well. Making mistakes simply means discovering that your undrerstanding of ideas and how to apply them is not perfect yet. More importantly, address the mistakes and learn from them.

LET MISTAKES HELP, NOT DESTROY

Change your beliefs about making mistakes. Successful students treat mistakes as signals that the strategies they have been using are not appropriate. As a result, they constantly keep changing their learning strategies till they reach a point of total preparation for the final examinations.

STUDENTS DO NOT FAIL, THEY MERELY GIVE UP TRYING

As long as you learn from our mistakes and failures and continually realign your strategies, you will ultimately succeed. However, if you give up trying because of your mistakes, then you would indeed have failed.

LESSONS ON LIFE

A man who knew no failure

Almost every great man or fabulously wealthy business person has reached where he or she is after setbacks that would have knocked out most other ordinary people. But the person whose life story inspired me most was a man who...

Was born in a log cabin to illiterate parents.
Had no formal education.
Had no positive role models.
Lost his mother at 9.
Failed in business at 22.
Defeated in an attempt to become a legislator at 32.
Dissolved another business at 25.
Experienced the death of his female companion at 26.
Was overcome with depression at 32.
Ran for congress and was defeated at 37.
Failed in an effort to become vice president at 47.
Lost a senatorial race at 49.
Was elected the 16th President of the United States at 51.

This man was Abraham Lincoln, one of the most respected presidents that ever lived. Despite repeated failures, Lincoln believed that he was worthy of greatness. To him, failure simply served as an indication that he must keep on changing his strategies and work harder till he finally he reached his greatest goal of all. So every time you make a mistake, think about this great man.

FORMULA 3: MAKE FULL USE OF TESTS & ASSIGNMENTS

Many students do not realize the importance of tests and assignments and consider them burdensome. Tests are in fact vital indicators of where you are now in your journey to realize your goals.

If you have failed every test, then it will be miraculous if you do well for the final examination. If you have consistently understood what you are studying and performed well at every milestone, then you can be quite sure of how you will do.

Before we can make full use of these tests, we must do two things, i.e. give the test our very best shot and do a post-mortem on each test.

1 DO YOUR BEST IN EACH TEST

It is only when we study for a test that we can analyze the results to reveal real weaknesses or confirm our strengths. Many students don't bother studying for tests, so when they get poor results, they cannot tell if their dismal performance was due lack of effort or insufficient comprehension of ideas.

2 DO A POST-MORTEM AFTER EACH TEST

Whether you do well or badly in a test, analyze your results in detail. If you did well, find out why. This helps you to recreate the same performance and obtain the same good results for the finals. If you did not score well, you need to isolate the reasons for your failure and ask yourself what you can do to ensure that it does not happen again.

DEALING WITH MISTAKES

Below, I have outlined three categories of common mistakes and solutions on how to ensure that they do not recur in the future.

Category 1: Carelessness

It was a careless mistake that you normally wouldn't make. You should address these mistakes by:

1. Practise working on more of the type of questions that cause you to stumble.
2. Check your answers when you have finished all other questions.
3. Be more attentive while answering the questions. Read each question carefully and bear it in mind as you work on the answers.

Category 2: Unforgivable Incapacity

You forgot the facts or simply did not study. To ensure that it does not recur, study thoroughly what you overlooked. If you had simply forgotten your facts, it was probably because you had either done insufficient revision or not applied the memory techniques properly.

Category 3: Genuine Inability

You genuinely could not give the right answer although you had studied hard. If your mistake falls into this category, then the question asked was probably unfamiliar to you. An examination usually consists of two or three of these difficult questions, meant to separate the 'A' grade students from the rest.

The only thing you can do is to find out how to arrive at the solution and practice aiming at it. It is important that you to expose yourself to as many of these difficult questions as possible. Work on more past-year examination papers, apart from those given by your teacher.

FORMULA 4:
THE ULTIMATE FORMULA FOR SCORING 'A'S

All the first three formulae along with what we have talked about so far can be summarized into an ultimate formula for academic success that you must apply in order to score A's.

1 Set A Specific Academic Goal.

We learned how to do this in the chapter on goal setting.

2 Take Action To Achieve That Goal.

Chapter Ten suggets how to take action consistently and overcome procrastination.

3 Be Flexible.

If you make mistakes or fail to get your outcome, change your strategy.

4 Take Action Again Till You Achieve Your Outcome.

There is no failure as long as you keep trying.

CHAPTER 12

TIME — OUR MOST PRECIOUS RESOURCE

What is the one precious thing that we lose a little bit of every second of our lives that does not seem to bother us? It is time. Time is valuable because you only have a limited amount of it before the examinations. Every strategy and action you need to take to help you do well in your examination requires time. Yet many students do not treasure their time. They do not realize that with each passing second, their examinations are getting nearer and nearer. In the end, they lament, saying, 'if only I had more time'.

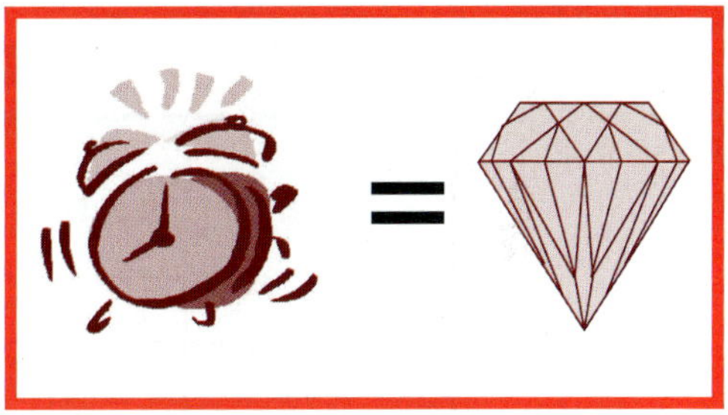

HOW MUCH TIME DO WE HAVE?

Students waste precious hours doing unproductive things because they think they have an abundance of time. Well, consider this. If you sleep an average of eight hours a day, every twenty-four hour day, it means that you will spend one-third of your life sleeping! If you were to live to eighty, you would effectively have spent twenty-seven years sleeping; in actual fact, you would have been consciously living for only fifty-three years. Does that seem like a lot of time to you?

HOW MUCH TIME DO YOU WASTE NOW?

Before you can appreciate time, it is important for you to realize how much time you waste each day. In the time grid below, fill in the activity you would normally be performing in the corresponding time slots given. For example, you may write down 'travelling home' as your activity at 5 pm.

In the column under 'Time wasted', write down the amount of time you lost during each of the activities you listed. An activity is considered a waste of time if it does not move you towards any of your goals, such as study goals, physical well-being goals, social goals and even spiritual ones. Activities not covered in these goals, like sleeping or visiting the bathroom, may be considered a waste of time if an inordinate amount of time is taken up in doing them. (e.g. sleeping for more than eight hours every day). Fill in the time sheet before you turn to the next page.

TIME GRID

Time	Activity	Time Wasted
6 am		
7 am		
8 am		
9 am		
10 am		
11 am		
12 pm		
1 pm		
2 pm		
3 pm		
4 pm		
5 pm		
6 pm		
7 pm		
8 pm		
9 pm		
10 pm		
11 pm		
12 am		
1 am		
2 am		

Now, add up the total time (in hours) you would normally waste in a day. Take this figure, assuming that this figure is six hours, and multiply it by three hundred-and-sixty-five days. This will give you the total number of hours you normally waste in one year. Next, multiply the figure by eighty years (assuming that your life expectation is eighty) and you will arrive at the total number of hours you could expect to waste in your lifetime.

Time wasted a day	=	6 hours
Time wasted in a year	=	Time wasted a day x 365 days
	=	6 hours x 365 days = 2190 hours
Time wasted in your lifetime	=	Time wasted in a year x 80 years
	=	2190 hours x 80 years
	=	175200 hours

This figure can easily be converted to years by dividing it by twenty four and then dividing it again by three hundred and sixty-five.

Time wasted in your lifetime	=	175200 hours
	=	175,200 ÷ 24 = 7300 days
	=	7300 ÷ 365 = 20 years

Assuming that you waste six hours a day on average (which is the norm), twenty years of your lifetime will be wasted. Think of what you could do with twenty-three years if you were to spend it productively!

MAKE TIME WORK FOR YOU

For you to make the best use of precious time, you must plan and manage your time daily. When you do this, you will discover, miraculously, that you will have more time to spend on studying and any other activities. You will never again say, 'I wish I had more time.' To plan your time, use a personal organizer which includes a monthly, weekly and daily calendar.

RULES IN PLANNING YOUR TIME

1 MAKE SPECIFIC PLANS

Your daily plans should include the day, the time and the duration of each activity.

2 * GIVE EACH ACTIVITY A PRIORITY STATUS *

When you have finished planning the time to be allocated to each activity, write down a priority status next to it. A red asterisk indicates that the activity is very important and cannot be delayed. It must be done on that specific day, at that specific time. A 'blue asterisk' indicates that the activity must be finished in that week.

3 DO NOT GO OVERBOARD ABOUT PLANNING

It is important that you be fair to yourself and plan only for what is necessary. If you find that you have finished early, reward yourself by relaxing or doing something else you enjoy. Incentives will encourage you to stick to your schedule.

4 STICK TO YOUR SCHEDULE

No matter what, you must finish the day's planned activities before you go to bed even if it means sleeping less or giving up your favourite programme. Self-denial will teach you the price you have to pay for wasting time and delaying your work.

But if, for a very important reason, you cannot stick to the planned activity, always make sure that you postpone it. Alternatively, swop it with a less demanding activity you have planned. But no matter what you do, never postpone it to the following week, otherwise you will end up with a huge pile of work, which will snowball.

5 MAKE USE OF EVERY MOMENT POSSIBLE

If you find that one day is too short for you to do much, then look again. There are small pockets of time during the day which could add up to a lot. If you make use of this time, you will be surprised at how much you can cover.

6 STRIKE OFF ACTIVITIES AS YOU COMPLETE THEM

As you finish each activity, strike it off your planner. This will give you a sense of accomplishment.

HOW FAR AHEAD DO I PLAN?

At the beginning of each year, list in your monthly calendar, the major activities in the coming year, dates of your examinations, school holidays and other major events. At the beginning of each month, update your calendar, making detailed plans for the coming month. At this stage, you should be able to include the dates of projects due for submission, class tests, class assignments and your social programmes. An illustration is given on the next page.

A MONTHLY CALENDER

June
1997

Sunday	Monday	Tuesday	Wednesday	Thursday	Friday	Saturday
1	2	3 Geography test today!	4	5 National holiday	6	7
8	9 Tennis Championship finals	10	11	12	13	14
15	16	17	18 Maths quiz today	19	20 Meet George at 5 p.m.	21
22	23 Susan's birthday	24	25 Science project due!!	26	27 History exams!	28
29	30 Physics exams!					

At the beginning of each week (every Sunday) you should mark in your weekly calender, details of what you intend to do, each day, for the coming week. Now is the time to plan for the days to be spent reading and doing Mind Maps® of certain chapters of your subjects, completing homework or projects assigned to you and on studying for upcoming tests.

A WEEKLY CALENDER

Week of

September 18 – October 1

28 — Sunday

- *Pre-read and do Mind Maps® for Geography chapter 3* *
- *Do Maths problems on page 12* *

29 — Monday

- *Read Act 5 of Macbeth* *

30 — Tuesday

- *Complete Science homework page 152* *
- *Do Maths assignments 2 and 3* *

1 — Wednesday

- *Study for coming History test* *
- *Prepare for Chemistry quiz* *

2 — Thursday

- *Discuss Geography project* *
- *Read and Mind Map® Science chapter 4* *

3 — Friday

- *Complete Science assignments on page 56* *

4 — Saturday

Finally, at the end of each day, make a very detailed daily plan of the activities you wish to undertake the next day. You may wish to include activities such as your study times, break times, times for your school lessons and recreation time, e.g. for watching television and playing video games.

Be very specific in the plans you make at this stage. You should indicate the exact time allocated to each activity you want to perform. Setting a specific time frame for each activity will prevent you from procrastinating. Again, an illustration is provided below.

A DAILY CALENDER

September 18, 1997
Thursday

Early	
8	*Jog & eat breakfast*
9	*Read newspapers, clean room and wash up*
10	*Prepare for History quiz* *
11	*Travel to school*
Noon	*Chemistry lesson*
1	*History lesson*
2	*Physical Education*
3	*Mathematics lesson*
4	*English Literature class*
5	*Travel home & clean up*
6	*Pre-read and Mind Map® Science, Chapter 9* *
7	*Do Maths assignment 4* *
8	*Break – Watch TV*
9	*Read Macbeth, Acts 4, 5* *
10	*Pre-read and Mind Map® The River Between, Chapter 11* *
11	*Break for supper and sleep*

MORE ON PLANNING

Here we focus on how you should plan your study-related activities. Do the same for other activities.

The most important study-related activities you have to plan for are:

1. of lesson materials and working on Mind Map®
2. homework, and working on class assignments
3. special projects, assignments and studying for tests that may arise

The days and times at which these activities will be carried out must be planned in conjunction with the days of your lessons in school and other extra-curricular activities. For example, if you are pre-reading a particular chapter on science, this must be done before the teacher covers that chapter during the lesson.

CHAPTER 13

FEEL EMPOWERED ALL THE TIME

TO SUCCEED, YOU MUST FEEL GOOD ABOUT YOURSELF!

You have learnt many techniques on how to learn more effectively, but does this mean that you will definitely go ahead and do it?

In fact, you may be saying to yourself right now, 'Yes, I know that I am supposed to set goals, do Mind Maps® and plan my time, but you know what? I just don't feel like doing it! I am too bored, tired and depressed'.

YOUR MENTAL STATES AFFECT YOUR BEHAVIOUR

Were there times before when you were totally excited and energized and felt that you could do anything? But were there also times when something depressed you and you just did not feel like doing anything?

Normally, we accept the states we get into and let them rule our behaviour and our lives. When we are bored and tired, we throw our books aside and flop down onto our beds and laze about. But to increase the quality of our lives, we must learn to control the states we get into.

YOU CREATE YOUR OWN MENTAL STATES

What you must begin to understand is that you are solely in control of whatever state you are in. So, no matter what happens to you, whether your girlfriend or boyfriend leaves you or whether you are have just been reprimanded by your parents, you can always put yourself into a totally energized, excited state to take positive action.

The techniques I am going to share with you on how to manage your own states come from the discipline of Neuro-Linguistic proramming (NLP). NLP was developed in 1972 by Dr. Richard Bandler and Dr. John Grinder and its domain lies in the study of the structure of subjective experience. NLP offers specific techniques which can be used by anyone to re-organize his or her subjective experience of the external world and hence create any behavioural outcome, such as the change of states and the elimination of phobias.

HOW ARE MENTAL STATES CREATED?

The kind of state you are in at any given moment depends on the way you are using your body as well as the kind of pictures, sounds and feelings you are making in your mind. The states you are in will affect the way you behave and ultimately the results you will produce. If you are always motivated, you will probably study harder and produce better results in school. So, in order for you to change your state, you must change the way you use your body and/or change the pictures, sounds and feelings you are creating in your mind.

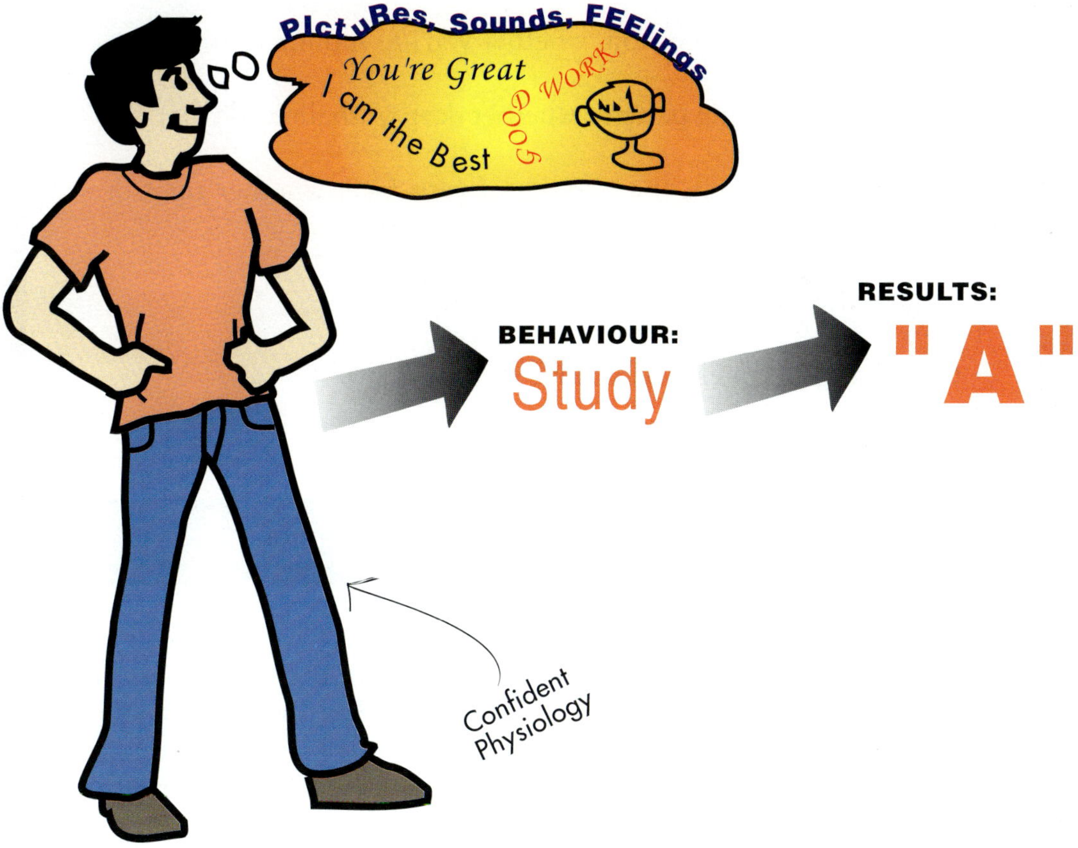

USING YOUR BODY TO CHANGE YOUR STATE

The way you use your body at any time will affect the state you are in. When I say use your body, I mean pay attention to:

1. your posture, whether you are slouching or throwing your shoulders back
2. your facial expression, whether you are smiling or frowning
3. your breathing pattern, whether deep or shallow, slow or fast
4. the tensions in the muscles of your face, whether tight or relaxed
5. the muscular tensions in your body
6. the tone, pitch and volume of your voice

In fact, the expression on your face right now, along with the way you are breathing and sitting, is affecting the way you are feeling now. What I would like you to do is to play along with me and join in the awareness raising exercises I will ask you to do. These exercises are aimed at getting you to note how posture, breathing and expression affect states.

GAME 1

Sit the way you would be sitting, breathe the way you would be breathing and look the way you would be looking if you were totally bored and tired. Now, in this position, I want you to notice where the position of your shoulders are. Is your breathing deep or shallow? What is the rest of your posture like? Are the muscles in your face tight or relaxed?

Go ahead and do this now.

Welcome back. Most of you would agree with me that your shoulders are drooping and that you are slouching and your breathing has slowed. Also, your facial muscles would probably have been droopy and you probably have a frown on your face. Isn't that interesting? Before we actually feel bored and tired, we must first use our bodies in a certain way. If not, there is no way we can feel bored and tired!

GAME 2

Let's try another experiment. I want you stand the way you would be standing, breathe the way you would be breathing and move your body as you would if you were totally excited and energized.

Now, while your body is in this totally powerful and energized state, I want you to try to feel depressed. Don't drop your shoulders and don't wipe off that smile! Don't cheat! Just breathe deeply, keep that big smile on your face, stand straight with shoulders back. In this position, try to feel bored and tired.

Go ahead and do this now.

Welcome back! Notice that if you did not change your posture and expression at all, there was no way you could have felt bored and tired. In order to have particular feelings, you must work your body in certain ways!

So. whenever you feel really lazy and bored and cannot get down to doing your schoolwork, simply stand tall and snap yourself into an empowering state by breathing fully, throwing your shoulders back and putting a big wide grin on your face. It will instantly change the way you feel and the way you behave.

This is a simple but extremely powerful concept! Practise snapping yourself into a powerful state whenever you feel tired, bored or depressed. The more you practise, the more automatic it will become. Pretty soon, every time you start to feel depressed, your mind will snap itself back into an excited state. Have fun doing it!

LESSONS ON LIFE

A piece of research done in the University of California some years ago involved a study on a group of people who were habitually depressed. These people had gone through years of therapy but nothing could be done to change their depressed state. However, when the researchers got these people to smile and to breathe more deeply, some of them, who had been depressed for years saw improvements in their mental health and their states.

USING YOUR MIND TO CHANGE YOUR STATE

There are only three things we can do with our mind. We can create images, and generate sounds and feelings in our mind's eye. What you choose to see, hear and feel in your mind will affect your state. For example, in order to be depressed, you have to:

picture unpleasant thoughts in your mind

For example, you could play back images of your parents shouting at you or picture the bad results you got last year.

create unpleasant sounds

For example, you could hear the voice of your worst enemy insulting you and putting you down. You could also hear your own inner voice going, 'you are good for nothing.'

choose to feel negative sensations

You could imagine feeling what it is like to be hurt by someone you care about.

So, the way to change your state at any time is to change the pictures, sounds and feelings you are creating in your mind at that moment. This NLP technique is thoroughly explained in *Using Your Brain For A Change*, by Dr. Richard Bandler.

CHANGING THE INTENSITY OF A STATE

It is useful for you to be able to intensify positive states like excitement and deintensify negative states like depression. Again, the way to do it is to change the pictures, sounds and feelings that are associated with those states.

For example, think of a time in the past when you felt totally confident and unstoppable. Perhaps it was a time when you scored an 'A' for a test or when you won a competition. Relive that experience by breathing deeply, throwing your shoulders back and putting a confident look on your face. See what you saw then, the sounds and voices around you that you heard and what you felt.

Do this now.

CHANGING THE PICTURES

As you think of that moment, I want you to notice the images you have created in your mind. Notice if the images are:

1. black-and-white or colour ____________
2. near or far ____________
3. bright or dim ____________
4. sharp or clear ____________
5. large or small ____________
6. part of a movie or are still shots ____________
7. associated or disassociated ____________
8. on the left, right, top or bottom of your mental screen ____________

*An associated image is one in which you are reliving an experience by looking through your own eyes. A disassociated image is one in which you are watching a movie of yourself, reliving an experience from a third person's perspective.

Now, I want you to play with that image in your mind. As you do so, notice if the feeling of confidence gets stronger or weaker. If your image is black-and-white, make it a rich colour. If your image is far away, bring it closer to your face. Similarly, if the image is dim and small, make it bigger and brighter. If you see a still image, turn it into a film. You can also change the location of the image on your mental movie screen. Lastly, if you are looking at yourself in the image, then step into your own body so that you become fully associated and are looking through your own eyes.

Do this now.

Welcome back. If you had played with your image, you would have noticed that it changed the way you felt. For most people, associating with the image and being able to make it bigger, brighter, closer and into a movie intensifies the feeling of confidence. Similarly, disassociating yourself from an image and making it small, dark and black-and-white removes its intensity.

CHANGING THE SOUNDS

Now, notice what sounds or voices you hear as you think about that time when you were totally confident. Perhaps it was the sound of a friend praising you. As you do, notice if the sounds or voices are:

1. fast or slow ____________
2. loud or soft ____________
3. pitched high or low ____________

Also ask yourself the following:

1. Where is the sound coming from? ____________
2. Is the sound muffled or sharp? ____________
3. What is the tonality? ____________
4. Is the rhythm regular or irregular? ____________

Write down the characteristics of the sound in the space given. Again, I want you to change the sounds in your mind. For example,you could bring the sound closer to you, make it sharper, more resonant, louder and more rhythmic.

STOP Do this now.

For most people, doing that would intensify the feelings of confidence. Similarly, if you wanted to deintensify the feelings of confidence, you could make the sound come from under your feet so that it is soft, muffled and irregular.

CHANGING THE FEELINGS

Next, I want you to concentrate on the feeling of confidence and make observations about it. Describe it as clearly as possible by providing the details required:

1. size ____________
2. location on your body ____________
3. shape ____________
4. weight ____________
5. intensity ____________

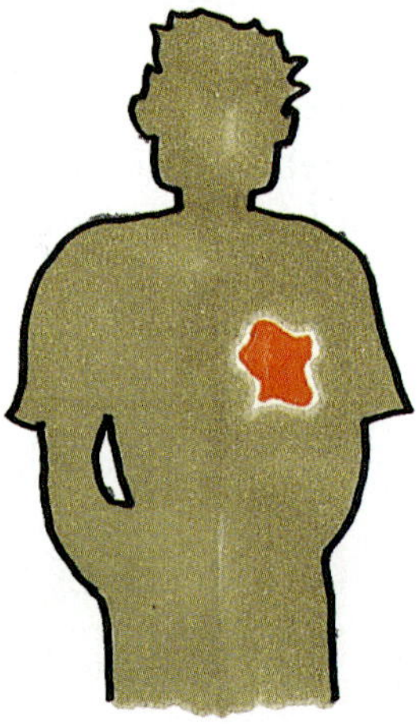

Now, experiment with those feelings. For example, you could increase the feeling of confidence by one hundred times, multiply the size of that feeling by ten times and change its location in your body.

STOP Do this now.

Good. Did that change your level of confidence? Now you can see how easy it is to change the intensity of a state. Let's take a look at more specific examples as we learn how to remove a negative mood and harnass a positive one.

REMOVING A NEGATIVE MOOD

Suppose someone or something depressed you. For example, let's say that a classmate insulted you this morning and you are still feeling really depressed about it. How would you cure your depression?

The way to do it would be to change the pictures, sounds and feelings you have about your classmate insulting you.

CHANGE THE PICTURE

So think about the image of your classmate insulting you this morning. First, disassociate yourself from the picture if you are currently looking at the whole episode through your perspective. Step out of your body, taking ten steps and pushing the picture further away until it is really small.

Now, take that image and turn down the intensity until it is very dim. Next, you can make the image very fuzzy. You can even be creative and imagine that little Mickey Mouse ears are growing on your classmate at the same time as his nose is swelling into a big red tomato. Finally put that small image in your hand, toss it towards the sun and see it explode into a million pieces.

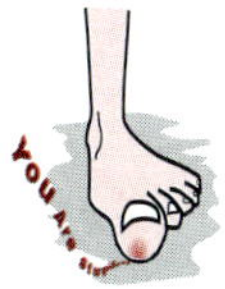

CHANGE THE SOUNDS & FEELINGS

Now, let your mind go back to school. Can you hear that offensive classmate's voice? Well, make that voice so squeaky that it sounds like a chipmunk's. Better still, turn down the volume so that you can only hear a faint sound. Finally, take that voice and put in under your big toe, so that your toe is 'talking' to you. Just by doing that, your thoughts about what happened that morning no longer have any effect on you. In fact, it may even make you laugh. If necessary, you can further remove the negative feelings by applying the same procedure.

HARNESSING A POSITIVE STATE

To put yourself into the right mood, simply think of a time in the past when you felt totally confident and motivated. It could be a time when you received an award, or when you accomplished a very difficult task.

As you think about that time, stand the way you stood on that occassion, breathe the way you did, and assume an expression of total confidence and motivation in your face. Good.

CHANGING THE PICTURES, SOUNDS AND FEELINGS

Now, take the images associated with that experience and make them bigger, brighter and sharper. Finally, turn the images into a movie. If you are currently disassociated, step into your body so that you are looking through your own eyes and are experiencing that moment as if it was happening right now.

Next, think about the sounds in that experience. Perhaps, these could be the sounds of hands cheering you on or those of encouraging voices from your friends and teachers. Make those sounds louder, clearer and more rhythmic. Imagine those sounds close to your ears so that they are just beside you. Lastly, take those feelings of confidence and motivation, multiply them by ten thousand times and securely place them right in the centre of your chest.

Do this now.

Well, how did that feel? I am sure you feel much more confident and motivated now. So, you can see that you have the ability to put yourself into a state of resourcefulness anytime you want to. It would be good for you to do this simple exercise before you go for an examination, a competition or any situation which requires you to feel confident and motivated.

You now have the ability to put yourself into the most powerful state required to take positive action. Turn the page to embark on a new chapter on examination preparation.

CHAPTER 14

THE FINAL COUNTDOWN

AS THE DAY OF THE EXAM DRAWS NEAR...

As examination day draws near, you will start to enter the final phase of your preparation. In this chapter, I will describe the entire process of how you can put yourself into an optimal state of preparedness for the examinations using all the concepts covered earlier.

By this time, you should have prepared Mind Maps® of all your relevant study materials. You should have also completed all assignments, projects and tests and clarified the mistakes made in them. The final preparation should comprise a revision of everything that you have covered, rather than a first time study of the material. It should not be your first effort at grappling with the material.

YOUR OBJECTIVE IS UNCONSCIOUS COMPETENCE

How is it that there are 'A' scorers, students who can complete their examination papers with time to spare and score 'A's while others simply run out of time? The answer lies in the difference of the level of competence that the two groups of students study to. Students who always run out of time merely study to a stage where they simply understand the subject, but are not adept or skilled at it. They still need time to think about and analyze a test question before answering it. This stage is known as the level of conscious competence.

Successful students, on the other hand, always study to a stage of unconscious competence. They revise their work to a stage where they can instinctively answer the questions without having to analyze the problem consciously. Their familiarity with the materials and methods helps them arrive at solutions quickly and competently.

Creating An

OPTIMAL LEARNING ENVIRONMENT

To study effectively, it is important for you to first create an optimal learning environment You should choose to study consistently at one place so your mind gets into the habit of working whenever you are there. The study area you choose should have the following characteristics:

Let There Be Light!

The environment most conducive to learning is one that is brightly lit, preferably with yellow light. This is because fluorescent (white) light is glaring and may lead to headaches.

Check The Temperature

A temperature that is too high will tend to make you feel drowsy. Try, as far as possible, to study in a place that is a little colder than what you would normally like. The reason is that a lower temperature will keep you more alert.

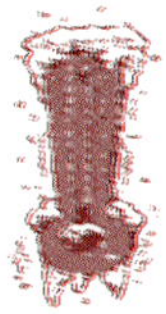

Free Yourself Of Distractions

Unless you have great discipline or willpower, always ensure that your study area is free from distractions like the TV, telephone, video games, comics or magazines or a bed.

Don't Pig Out!

Do not eat a big meal before a study session. It often makes you drowsy because a lot of your energy and blood is directed to your digestive system. This makes it difficult to cope with the extra food. Try to avoid red meat (burgers), sugar or white flour (found in cakes and pastry) before studying, as these food types reduce your brain's ability to store information.

Bach For Background Music?

Play music in the background whenever you study. Music is rhythmic and listening it has a synergistic effect which enhances brain power. The best kind of music to use in learning is Baroque music because it maintains rhythm of sixty beats per minute which puts the mind in a relaxed state (alpha state) so that learning can take place.

Individual Or Group Study?

Is it better to study alone or in a group? It depends. Group study allows you to pool resources and knowledge. However, if you choose to work with students who are ill-disciplined, you will be distracted. So, always approach those who are more resourceful and more disciplined than you. In this way, you can only be influenced for the better.

Individual study, on the other hand, guarantees minimal distraction. But it also means that you will not be able to share and compare notes with other students.

The bottom line is that you should study individually, and, at times, arrange group study sessions.

PLAN A STUDY SCHEDULE EARLY

About two months prior to the examinations, draw up a detailed study schedule of what you intend to study each day, right up to the day your first paper begins. This will ensure that you cover all the necessary subjects on time.

How Early Should We Start Preparation?

Work backwards from the date of your first paper. You must calculate how much time you will need to effectively cover all the subjects involved. Try to allocate five days for emergencies that may crop up. However, always imagine that the five extra days do not exist, or you may be tempted to procrastinate.

How Much Time Should Be Allocated To Each Subject?

Although the amount of time you should allocate to each subject is unique from person to person, you could follow these guidelines:

1 SPREAD OUT STUDY ON A PARTICULAR SUBJECT

Instead of cramming the study of a particular subject, like Geography, over a few days, it is better to study just one to two chapters each day over a longer period of time, say ten days. Spreading the study of a subject over a few days ensures that your mind has time to digest the information and organize it before moving on to another 'chunk' of information.

2 PLAN FOR DAILY STUDY SESSIONS

Remember that in order to achieve the greatest number of high points of recall, you should always plan a study session of up to a maximum of two hours. After each study session, wait for at least half an hour before starting another session. Within each study session, always take a break of between two and five minutes.

Your study sessions should be divided into four separate periods of not more than twenty-five minutes each. During each study break, your mind should be as relaxed as possible.

3 PLAN FOR THIRD AND FOURTH REVISIONS

You also need to schedule revision times for subject. Remember that to keep your memory in an optimal condition, you have to revise whatever you have learnt within ten minutes, twenty-four hours, a week and a month. The first two revisions (i.e. within ten minutes and twenty-four hours), are normally done in the study sessions you have already planned for. You only need to make additional study slots for the third and fourth (if necessary) revisions of every subject. I suggest that the fourth revision of a particular subject (like physics) be planned on the day before that particular paper.

STUDYING DURING A STUDY SESSION

As mentioned earlier, a two-hour study session should be sufficient time to cover a subject chapter of average length. For slightly longer chapters, you may need to use two study sessions. For each study session, you should cover the following:

Revise The Previous Day's Work Ideally, you should be able to re-create in your mind the entire Mind Map® based on the chapter you reviewed the day before, without referring to your notes. You must also review the homework assigned to that particular chapter.

Go Through The Day's Materials For the day's chapter of study, go through your Mind Maps® thoroughly and then use the memory systems like the Link System and the Number System to commit the key points to memory.

Go Through The Homework Assignments Besides going through the study material, you must practise doing your homework assignments questions again, and then check the answers. By re-doing the assignments, you are installing the knowledge into the level of unconscious competence.

Do An Overall Revision Of Today's Material This should take you no more than ten minutes. Remember that you should always revise when your memory peaks ten minutes after each study period.

A STUDY SCHEDULE

An illustration is given of how you can create a study schedule for yourself, using all the concepts we have discussed so far. In this illustration, I will assume that the following subjects will be included in your final examinations:

Subject	Abbreviation	Number Of Chapters	Examination Date
Mathematics	Maths	10	18 November
Geography	Geog	12	28 November
History	History	10	22 November
Physics	Physics	12	24 November
Chemistry	Chem	10	25 November
Literature	Lit	12	27 November

The study schedule is presented in the following two pages. In particular, note that in planning the schedule:

1. A five-day buffer (13 to 17 November) is given for emergencies, although revisions are planned within them.

2. We start by working backwards from the day labelled 'End Of Study'. This day is the first day of the buffer period.

3. A final review, normally the fourth revision, is done on the day before each paper. For example, the final history review takes place on 21 November, which is the day before the History exam.

4. As far as possible, a mix of different subjects is planned for each day's study.

5. Before starting each day's work, a revision (within twenty-four hours) is done on subjects studied the previous day. This is indicated with an asterisk.

6. If one week has passed since you last studied a particular subject, do an overall revision of the entire subject.

A STUDY SCHEDULE (I)

October
1997

Sunday	Monday	Tuesday	Wednesday	Thursday	Friday	Saturday
			1	2	3	4
5	6	7	8	9	10	11
12	13	14	15	16 *Start of preparation*	17 *Physics 1, 2, 3*	18 * *Physics 4, 5, 6*
19 * *Physics 7, 8, 9*	20 * *Maths 1* *History 1* *Physics 10*	21 * *Maths 2* *History 2* *Physics 11*	22 * *Maths 3* *History 3* *Physics 12*	23 * *Maths 4* *History 4*	24 * *Maths 5* *History 5*	25 * *Maths 6* *History 6*
26 * *Maths 7* *History 7*	27 * *Maths 8* *History 8*	28 * *Overall Physics Revision (1 week)*	29 * *Maths 9* *History 9*	30 * *Maths 10* *History 10*	31 * *Geog 1* *Lit 1* *Chem 1*	

A STUDY SCHEDULE (II)

November
1997

Sunday	Monday	Tuesday	Wednesday	Thursday	Friday	Saturday
30						1 * Geog 2 Lit 2 Chem 2
2 * Geog 3 Lit 3 Chem 3	3 * Geog 4 Lit 4 Chem 4	4 * Geog 5 Lit 5 Chem 5	5 * Geog 6 Lit 6 Chem 6	6 * Geog 7 Lit 7 Chem 7	7 * Overall Maths Revision Overall History Revision (1 week)	8 * Geog 8 Lit 8 Chem 8
9 * Geog 9 Lit 9 Chem 9	10 * Geog 10 Lit 10 Chem 10	11 * Geog 11 Lit 11	12 * Geog 11 Lit 12 End of Study	13 * ← Extra 5 days (for emergencies) →	14	15
16 * Overall Chem Revision (1 week)	17 * Final Maths Review	18 Maths Exam	19 * Overall Lit Revision (1 week)	20 * Overall Geog Revision (1 week)	21 * Final History Review	22 * History Exam
23 * Final Physics Review	24 Physics Exam Final Chem Review	25 Chem Exam	26 Final Lit Review	27 Lit Exam Final Geog Review	28 Geog Exam	29

CHAPTER 15

THE FINAL BATTLE

Although it is almost a guarantee that a well prepared student will pass well, it may take more than preparedness to score distinctions. This is because well prepared students may not produce their best work under the stressful conditions of an examination. In this chapter, I will be pointing out some of the more common mistakes that students make under examination pressure. We will also look at precautions you can take to ensure that you give your best, on this all-important day.

It is always good to arrive early for an examination. Firstly, it guarantees that you will be able to finish the paper and secondly, being early allows your mind to relax before it is put to work. Remember that your mind performs at its best when you are in a relaxed state. It will definitely help if you could chat with your friends about anything that could take your mind off studying, but never talk about the examination or the study material.

Most of all, never ever study on the day of the examination. This is the best way to sabotage your mind. Doing so will put you in a more tense state and the new material could only confuse you and interfere with any information that your mind has so well sorted out and integrated during your sleep.

SCAN THE TEXT

The first thing you should do when you start the paper is to read through all the instructions and scan the entire paper from beginning to end before starting to attempt any questions. Scanning helps you to plan the order in which to answer the questions as well as how much time to spend on each section.

A WORD ON TIME

A lack of time is the undoing of many students, whether they are prepared or not. So it is important that you keep track of the time by glancing at your watch every time you feel the need to. In order to avoid running out of time, you should:

Allocate Your Time Wisely Always plan in advance the amount of time you will spend on each section and, subsequently, on each question. This should mostly be done during your dry runs.

Plan For Extra Time You should also plan for an extra 'check-back time' of at least fifteen minutes. This time can also be used as an emergency measure, if you happen to exceed the time you've allocated for your questions.

APPROACHING THE QUESTIONS

Easy First, Difficult Last

It is not always a good idea to answer the questions in the sequence in which they are found. This is because, at times, very difficult questions may be put in the beginning while easier ones are at the end. When we get we may continue trying till we find that we have spent too much time on it. Consequently, we rush through the rest of the paper only to find that we have no more time left to do even the easy questions. The consequence is failure. To avoid this, you should do either one of the following:

1. Whenever you find that you are stuck with a difficult question, immediately circle that difficult question and go on to the next one. You can return to it after you have finished answering all the easy ones.

2. Answer all the easy questions first before proceeding with the difficult ones. Always leave the ones that require a lot of thinking, analysis and writing to the end, when you have finished most of the paper. This is because these are often best done when your mind is in a more relaxed state.

Don't Get Carried Away

Very often, students get so excited about answering a familiar question that they write on and on until they find that they have wasted too much time on it. Avoid giving too much information.

Never Give Up

Difficult questions, especially if they are put at the beginning of a paper, often have the effect of demoralizing you. When this happens, you will probably not even be able to answer the easy questions that come later on because you would have formed the belief that it was a difficult paper that you could not handle.

If this happens to you, take a deep breath, relax and do not give up. Skip the problematic questions and tackle the easy ones that would boost your confidence. When you go back to the difficult questions finally and find that you still cannot figure out the answers, never leave the answer space blank because that will guarantee you a zero for that question.

Instead, write down whatever you do know as long as it contains a germ of logic. Not only have you nothing to lose but you may still be awarded with some marks and that could make the difference between a pass or a fail mark.

ANSWERING THE QUESTIONS

There are two rules you should following in answering any kind of question. They are:

Always Read Critically

Always read each question slowly and carefully before attempting to answer it. Students often read the first few words and assume that the question is the same as one that they have done before, in earlier tests and homework. You may end up giving an answer that is totally off the point.

Remember that it takes only one word to change the meaning of an entire question. If we do not read carefully, we may miss that crucial word and misunderstand the whole question. So always be alert to critical key words that appear in the question.

For example, do not read 'and' where the questions say 'or'. Also, do not confuse 'which of the following statements are true' with 'which of the following statements are <u>not true</u>'.

Give The Right Amount Of Information

Never dive into a question without knowing what is actually required. If you do so, you may give too little information, too much information or information that is totally irrelevant.

The first step is to know how much information to give. The marks allotted to each question is often a very good gauge. If a question is awarded five marks then you would normally be required to produce five points, and so on.

Now, let's take a look at how you should answer specific categories of questions like the multiple choice and the essay.

YOUR FINAL MOMENTS

After you finish answering all the questions, you should ideally have fifteen minutes left to spare, as you had initially planned. It is vital that this time be used to double-check on your answers. You will definitely begin to see some errors you have made in understanding the questions, or giving the answers. It is also now that you will begin to see facts which you may have forgotten to put down.

So how do we double-check answers? Double-checking in the last twenty minutes should include the list provided across the page:

1. Re-read the questions to make sure that you have understood them correctly.

2. Re-read your essay and short-question type answers and make sure these answers are to the point and free from grammatical and spelling errors. Also ensure that no important points have been left out.

3. If time permits, recalculate (preferably using an alternative method) all mathematical questions to see if you get the same answer. If you are short of time, simply read through your workings.

4. As for multiple-choice questions, check that you have not missed any of them out. More importantly, when the answers are given in a separate answer booklet, check that the answers you have given correspond to the correct questions. Lastly, never leave any question unanswered.

YOUR DESTINY IS YOURS TO CREATE

Well, you have certainly come down a long road, haven't you, whoever you are and wherever in the world you are. In the moments you have spent reading the book, you have learnt many simple, yet powerful concepts that can change the way you study, forever. You have realized that the beliefs you have about who you are and what you can do will ultimately determine the results you produce. You know that if other students can achieve good results, then so can you. It is only a matter of acquiring the skills and strategies. You also now know about the infinite capacity of your brain. You realize that given the right keys, you can access the genius within you. You have learnt what these keys are, haven't you? You are cognisant of how to use both sides of your brain using techniques like Mind Mapping® and the Memory systems which you can put into effect to create the compelling future that you have planned for yourself and which you read about in the chapter on goal setting. You are capable of self-motivation and have turned into a competent time manager. Procrastination is not for you!

I urge you to take action now, as you turn the final page of this book. Take out your school textbooks, create a few Mind Maps® and use the memory techniques to see how fun and easy learning can be. Use your diary to plan your time for the coming week. You may even want to write in your journal more empowering goals for the future.

Remember, just because you have not done well in school in the past does not mean that you will not do well in the future. The success of your future depends on what you do today. So, go out there and start to plant the seeds for an abundant harvest.

Finally, I wish you all the very best in your journey to success. I hope that you will write to me or that if we will meet one day at a seminar you will tell me your success story.

Until then, be sure to live your dreams!

Adam Khoo

BIBLIOGRAPHY

Bandler, R. & Grinder, J. (1975). *The Structure Of Magic II*. California: Meta Publications.

Bandler, R. (1993). *Time For A Change*. California: Meta Publications.

Bandler, R. (1985). *Using Your Brain For A Change*. Utah: Real People Press.

Buzan, T. (1989). *How To Make The Most Of Your Mind*. Cambridge: Colt Books.

Buzan, T. (1993). *The Mind Map® Book*. London: BBC.

Buzan, T. (1989). *Use Your Memory*. London: BBC.

Covey, S. R. (1989). *The 7 Habits of Highly Effective People*. New York: Fireside.

Dilts, R. (1983). *Applications Of Neuro-Linguistic Programming*. California: Meta Publications.

Dilts, R. (1990). *Changing Belief Systems With NLP*. California: Meta Publications.

Dilts, R., Grinder, J., Bandler, R. and Delozier, J. (1980). *Neuro-Linguistic Programming: Volume I*. California: Meta Publications.

Jensen, E. (1995). *Brain Based Learning and Teaching*. San Diego: Turning Point Publishing.

Jensen, E. (1995). *Super Teaching*. San Diego: Turning Point Publishing.

Mukerjea, D. (1997). *Superbrain*. Singapore: Oxford University Press.

O'Conner, J. & Seymour, J. (1994). *Training with NLP: Skills for Managers, Trainers and Communicators*. California: Harper Collins Publishers.

Ostrander, S. & Schroeder, L. (1984). *Super-Learning 2000*. New York: Dell Publishing.

Ostrander, S. and Schroeder, L. (1991). *Super-Memory, The Revolution*. New York: Carrol & Graff.

Ostrander, S. and Schroeder, L. (1991). *Cosmic Memory*. New York: Carrol & Graff.

Robbins, A. (1988). *Unlimited Power*. Great Britain: Simon & Schuster.

Robbins, A. (1991). *Awaken The Giant Within*. New York: Summit Books.

Rose, C. (1987). *Accelerated Learning*. New York: Dell.

Rose, C. & Nicholl, M. J. (1984). *Accelerated Learning For The 21st Century*. New York: Dell Publishing.

Shone, S. (1984). *Creative Visualisation*. London: The Aquarian Press.

I AM GIFTED, SO ARE YOU!
SEMINAR SERIES

I. HOLIDAY PROGRAMMES FOR STUDENTS

1. The Super-Teen® Holiday Camp (five days-residential)
2. The Super-Teen® Weekend Experience (two days)

* *Super-Teen® programmes are currently available in Singapore, Malaysia and Hong Kong.*

II. PUBLIC & IN-HOUSE TRAINING PROGRAMMES

For Teachers and Trainers

1. Revolutionary Trainer's Training (three days)
2. Advanced Communication Mastery (two days)

For Students

1. Personal & Examination Mastery (three days)
2. Academic Memory Mastery (two days)
3. Mind Talk & Personal Motivation (two days)
4. Accelerated Reading Mastery (two days)
5. Communication Mastery (one day)
6. Formal Excellence: How To Develop Your EQ (two days)

For Parents

1. Effective Parenting (2 days)

* *Courses are currently available in Singapore In-house courses can be tailored to the needs of educational institutions.*

All programmes are designed by Adam Khoo or Ernest Wong and are conducted and facilitated by experienced trainers who have been trained in the United States by Dr. Richard Bandler, Dr. Tad James, Robert Dilts or John La Velle, world class Master-Trainers of Neuro-Linguistic Programming.

For feedback, questions or a free brochure, please contact:

In Singapore

ADAM KHOO

Executive Trainer, Ernesco Pte Ltd
Mailing Address: 9 Jalan Mariam, Singapore 509296
Tel/Fax: (65)5424367
email: Adamkhoo@hotmail.com
GSM: (65)96855408

THERESA WONG

Programme Manager, Ernesco Pte Ltd.
Mailing Address: 122 Middle Road, #07-04 Midlink Plaza, Singapore 188973
Tel: (65)4530768
Fax: (65)4523218
email: Superteenprog@hotmail.com

In Malaysia

ERNEST WONG

Principal Consultant, Ernesco Sdn Bhd.
Mailing Address: 71A Jalan Jajaka, Taman Maluri, Cheras 55100 Kuala Lumpur, Malaysia.
Tel: (03)9813136
Fax: (03)9813126

OTHER FOLLOW-UP RESOURCES

1. Seminars & Training Programmes

Buzan Centres (S) Pte Ltd
Orchard Post Office
P.O. Box 706
Singapore 912324
Tel : (65) 447 1866
Fax: (65) 466 2547

Buzan Centres UK
54 Parkstone Road
Poole, Dorset BH15 2PX, UK
Tel : (441) 20267 4676
Fax: (441) 20267 4776

The First Institute Of NLP™ & DHE™
268 Bush Street Suite
4115 San Francisco
CA 94104
Tel : (141) 5882 4657
Fax: (141) 5974 0349

Advanced Neuro Dynamics
1833 Kalakaua Avenue Suite 908
Honolulu, HI 96815
Tel : (808) 1800-800-6463

NLP University
P.O. Box 1112, Ben Lomond
California 95005, USA
Tel : (408) 336 3457
Fax: (408) 336 5854

Trans Neuro-Technologies & Universal Learning Dynamics Education Services
570 Macpherson Road #13-01
Singapore 368237
Tel : (65) 842 2453
Fax: (65) 560 5043

2. Books, Tapes and Other Materials

Optimum Performance Technologies
420 North Bridge Road
#03-12 North Bridge Centre
Singapore 188727
Tel : (65) 334 3605
Fax: (65) 569 8721

Success City
11 North Bridge Road
#01-44 Peninsula Plaza
Singapore 179098
Tel : (65) 334 2239
Fax: (65) 338 5719

Meta Publications
P.O. 1910, Capitola
CA 95010, USA
Tel : (408) 464 0254
Fax: (408) 464 0517